Rough Shooting

ROUGH SHOOTING
Third Edition

Mike Swan

SWAN·HILL PRESS

First published in the UK in 1991
by Swan Hill Press, an imprint of Quiller Publishing Ltd
    Reprinted 1994, 1997
2nd edition published in 2000
    Reprinted 2002
This 3rd edition pubished 2007

British Library Cataloguing-in-Publication Data
    A catalogue record for this book
    is available from the British Library

ISBN 978 1 84689 010 9

Typeset by Phoenix Typesetting, Auldgirth, Dumfriesshire.
Printed in China   .

Swan Hill Press
an imprint of Quiller Publishing Ltd
Wykey House, Wykey, Shrewsbury, SY4 1JA
Tel: 01939 261616 Fax: 01939 261606
E-mail: info@quillerbooks.com
Webste: www.countrybooksdirect.com

Contents

Acknowledgements   10

Foreword by Jonathan Young, editor of *The Field*   11

Introduction   13

Section 1 – Getting Started   17

  1 Basic Woodcraft   19
      Remaining unobtrusive 19
      Moving stealthily   21
      When to wait   21
      What's about?   22

  2 Quarry Recognition   24
      Knowing your way around 24
      Binoculars and field guides 24
      Joining a group   25
      Points to look for   25

  3 The Rough Shooter's Dog   27
      The need for a dog   27
      The dog's duties   28
      Choosing the right dog 29
      Caring for your dog   32
      Training your dog   32

  4 Guns and Cartridges   35
      The shotgun and how it works 35
      Suitable cartridges   38
      Non-toxic loads   39
      Suitable guns   40
      Proof   43
      Gun care and cleaning 43
      Safe gun handling   44

5 Clothes and Equipment 46
    Staying warm, dry and comfortable 46
    Hearing protection 48
    Safety glasses 49
    Game-bags and cartridge belts 49
    Knives, calls and other gadgets 50

6 Legal and Ethical Considerations 53
    Possession of guns 53
    Repeating and semi-automatic guns 54
    Rights to shoot 54
    Quarry lists and open seasons 55
    Sunday shooting 57
    Game licences 58
    Non-toxic shot 58
    Selling game 58
    Insurance protection 58
    Respect for the quarry 59
    The other person's sport 59
    The public perception 60
    The Code of Good Shooting Practice 60

Section 2 – Quarry and their Pursuit 61

7 Pheasants 63
    Origins 63
    Natural history 65
    Walked-up pheasants 67
    Hedges and ditches 67
    Big woods 69
    Small drives 71
    Stops and beaters 73
    Cocks only 73

8 Partridges 75
    Origins 75
    Natural history 75
    Habits 78
    Walking-up 78
    Small drives 81
    Shootable stocks 83

9 Woodcock 85
    Natural history and migration 85
    Woodcock shooting 89

	Walking-up	89
	Small drives	91
	Flighting	91

10	Snipe	94
	Natural history and migration	94
	Snipe shooting	96
	Walking-up	96
	Driving	97
	Flighting	99
	Shot sizes	99

11	Ground Game	101
	The humble bunny	101
	The leaping hare	103
	Shooting rabbits and hares	104
	Rough cover and bunnies	105
	Walked-up hares	106
	Driving	106
	Over ferrets	107
	Shot size and safety	108

12	Wildfowl	110
	Migration patterns	111
	Flighting patterns	112
	Feeding behaviour	113
	Morning flight	118
	Evening flight	120
	Daytime flight	122
	Moonflighting	123
	Walking-up	123
	Driving	124

13	Pigeons	126
	Natural history	126
	Food choice and crop damage	128
	Shooting over decoys	130
	Summer along the hedgerows	132
	Winter evenings and roost shooting	132

14	Principles of Decoying	135
	Of ducktraps and other shams	135
	The qualities of a good decoy	136
	Decoy patterns	138
	Successful siting of decoys	139

Pulling power   141
Eye catchers   142
Decoy shyness   143
Remaining hidden   143

Section 3 – Managing the Shoot   147

15   Conservation and Restocking Policy   149
     Good habitat   149
     Wild versus reared   150
     Do we add pheasants?   151
     The value of variety   152

16   Habitat Management   154
     Improving the woods   154
     Managing the hedges   156
     Open country   158
     Marshes and ponds   158
     Conservation and game management   160

17   Predation Control   164
     Why control predators?   164
     Which predators cause most damage?   165
     Avian predators   165
     Ground predators   167
     Fox control   167
     Smaller ground predators   169

18   Continuing Care   170
     Leaving a healthy stock   170
     Food in winter   171
     Joining the crowd   173

Appendix I: The Fieldsports Organisations   175

Appendix II: The Quarry in Death   177

Bibliography   179

Index   183

Dedication

For Cloth Ears, who has given more in seven seasons than one can
reasonably ask of a canine lifetime.

Acknowledgements

This book has been some time in the preparation, and a considerable number of people have helped. The basic concept of a kind of 'one man and his dog' guide to rough shooting was the thought of my old chum Colin McKelvie. His guiding hand and expert advice throughout the writing have been a great help.

I would never have been involved with fieldsports writing were it not for my job. The Game Conservancy Trust is a tremendously stimulating place to work, and is full of thoughtful and enthusiastic people. My colleagues there have provided a continuous background of expert comment and constructive ideas. For help with this book I am particularly grateful to Charles Nodder, Dick Potts, Steve Tapper, Pete Robertson, Maureen Woodburn, Judy Pittock, Kevin Wissett-Warner and Andrew Hoodless. I also offer special thanks to my secretary, Liz Scott, who has deciphered my scrawl and typed every word, as well as the endless corrections. Other people outside The Game Conservancy Trust have helped in their particular field too, and my grateful thanks go to Charlie Parkes, John Thornley, John Batley and Martin Deeley.

Jonathan Yule has become a great friend since I bought my first picture from him over five years ago. His splendid sketches add an atmosphere to the book which words alone could never convey. I am also fortunate to have been able to draw on The Game Conservancy Trust's photographic library for many of the illustrations. This has been built up from so many people's work that it is impossible for me to know who produced every last picture. In more recent years many of Terence Blank's photographs have been lodged at The Game Conservancy Trust, and I am grateful to his widow for permission to use some of them. My old friends John Marchington and Ian Grindy have been generous in supplying other photographs: the rest are largely my own work, although Maureen Woodburn has been kind enough to take some for me while I 'posed' and did the necessary.

My first article, under the series 'Shoot on a Shoestring' appeared in *Shooting Times* in 1982. Since then I have had great support from that magazine, and the then editor Jonathan Young has become a good friend. I am extremely grateful to him for writing the foreword to this book and for valuable comments on the draft manuscript.

It would have been impossible for me to contemplate writing this book but for the wide range of shooting which I have had as the guest of so many friends. Participation in shooting brings with it a camaraderie which I have never met in any other sport save perhaps angling, and I am grateful for so many happy times shared with so many good people. I shall always remember those crisp winter mornings when we set out together, guns under arms and dogs bouncing alongside, in eager anticipation of what was to follow.

Mike Swan
Fordingbridge
Hampshire

Foreword

by Jonathan Young, editor of *The Field*

This book is about 40 yards, the effective range of a shotgun. It is not a great distance for our quarry species: a pheasant, teal or wood pigeon can cover it in seconds. But for the hunter stalking a rabbit behind a tussock or pigeon in a roost wood that 40 yards is measured inch by inch. Almost as carefully, indeed, as it is gauged by a bunch of wigeon as they swirl into the decoys, sense something wrong, and pull away before the shot can be taken.

Getting within range of your quarry is an art that cannot be acquired at a shooting school. No one can quite explain how a duck tenses just before it springs or how one patch of bog feels snipey and another does not: fieldcraft requires lots of time in fields.

There are shortcuts though, if you are lucky enough to have a friend who is a natural hunter and teacher. I am extremely lucky: Mike Swan is my friend. His hunting skills are highly impressive. Outwitting woodcock and fooling pheasants is easy for him. His fieldsports knowledge is encyclopaedic, as you would expect from the Technical Information Officer of The Game Conservancy Trust.

This book is based on Mike Swan's practical experience. It does not cover moorland game because he considers himself insufficiently qualified. He gives first-class advice on all aspects of lowland rough shooting because he has done it and done it well.

Getting within 40 yards of our quarry will never be easy; if it were we would give up shooting. But this book helps.

Introduction

'I do feel strongly that . . . the main consideration should not be the mass slaughter of birds but rather the pursuit of that truer happiness which comes to those who shoot for love of the countryside and of all wildlife. I think that this applies even more in wildfowling and rough shooting than in other branches.'

Ian Pitman *And Clouds Flying* (1947)

The rough shooting ethos

Rough shooting is often considered a poor man's sport which is somehow distinctly inferior to shooting driven game. It is, of course, true that the most expensive type of game shooting is usually the driven day – if only because he who stands at a peg or butt will perforce have to employ others to bring his game to him. In many cases, the bag expectation is likely to be higher too, and this cannot be achieved without cost in terms of keeping and management. Whether or not all this means that the driven shot gets more enjoyment or excitement is a moot point.

Personally I like to look upon the two branches of our sport as having two slightly separate aims. Driven game shooting is, or at least should be, above all a test of marksmanship, with high or fast-flying birds to stretch to shooter's skill. Rough shooting by its very nature is much less of a test of this particular skill. This is not to suggest that the roughshooter need not be a good shot, but rather that not all of his chances will be high and fast. On the other hand, the rough shooter will in some senses need to be a more complete sportsman in that he will largely be responsible for making his own sport. If he does not know where to find his quarry his chances of success will be much reduced.

In continental Europe, America and indeed most other countries there is a much stronger tradition of the hunter or chasseur with dog and gun making his own sport alone, or perhaps with a chosen companion. To him a comparatively small bag is quite acceptable. The challenge of having woodcraft to match marksmanship, so that he is able both to find and to shoot his quarry brings its own satisfaction.

Having the right companion can add immeasurably to the day, but even when he hunts by himself the rough shooter is not alone. He has the companionship of his dog and of course also of the wilderness and its inhabitants. If he is to do well he must be a good naturalist, for he must understand his quarry and its habitat, and be able to recognise the signs which indicate its presence when it is not immediately obvious.

The sum of all this means that, in many senses, the actual shooting is far less important – there is so much to see and do that squeezing the trigger almost takes second place. There will, of course be memorable shots, but most rough shooters will not object too strongly to taking an easy one, especially if it represents the culmination of an hour or more of hard work. It might perhaps be the only chance of the day.

For the rough shooter then, there is much more to the sport than just shooting. His satisfaction comes from the whole countryside and what it contains and from harvesting for his own pot a little of what nature offers. He will not be entirely disappointed if he shoots nothing, especially if he comes across enough mushrooms to make tomorrow's breakfast.

Exactly what constitutes rough shooting will vary according to the sportsman's point of view. For this book I have taken limits based on three criteria. Firstly, the rough shooter is basically an opportunist. He rarely has a completely fixed and inflexible plan. Most sport will be walked-up, but I have deliberately included waiting for sport to come to the Gun too. So, secondly, the complete rough shooter should be able to identify when the best sport is likely to be provided by pigeons or wildfowl coming to him. Therefore, I have included a few notes on pigeons, ducks and geese, and on the use of hides and decoys. Some would say that this is a different sport, but I feel that the two approaches grade imperceptibly into one another.

The third criterion is that when the Gun stands at a peg or butt all day he ceases to be a roughshooter. However, this does not mean that roughshooting does not include an element of driving. The sort of shoot where a small group of Guns take turn and turn about to stand at the end of a covert, or to drive it, is at least half-way to being a rough shoot. The team still need to have woodcraft and dogs which measure up to their shooting abilities if the day is to be a success.

I have left out the question of grouse and moorland shooting completely. The reason for this is simple; lack of experience. While I have been lucky enough to shoot over other peoples' dogs, I have never worked pointers or setters, and the numbers of grouse and ptarmigan which I have shot are very few. It would therefore be quite wrong for me to try to write in detail about such matters.

This book therefore is about lowland rough shooting – the pursuit of small game in woods, fields, marshes and pools with a shotgun. I have assumed a little basic knowledge on the part of my readership. To have started from the very beginning would have made for an impossibly long text. In particular, I have assumed that my readers have shot before – if only at clays. To try to teach how to shoot is really outside the scope of a work like this – there are other books on the subject, and beginners will need a little personal coaching from an instructor or a clay shooting club anyway. So, I have written this book with those in mind who have dabbled a little in shooting and want to know more.

Section 1
GETTING STARTED

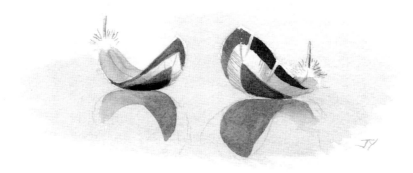

1

Basic Woodcraft

'The essence of stalking roe deer, whether the object is to shoot them or take their picture, is to outwit a wary adversary on its own ground.'

Richard Prior *Modern Roe Stalking* (1988).

Remaining unobtrusive

An amazing number of chances for a shot are lost, often with the Gun blissfully unaware, because of ineptitude. Far too many people clump noisily through the woods and fields with no thought for whether this is the right approach. In some cases, such as when driving pheasants, some degree of noise is a help, although even here too much is a hindrance. At the other end of the scale, wildfowl loafing in a ditch or pool are likely to depart long before a Gun is in shot unless he approaches with considerable stealth so as to remain both unseen and unheard.

The first thing to understand is that it is easy to be obtrusive when necessary – being unobtrusive is far more difficult. He is a wise Gun who trains his dog to whistles and gestures rather than to voice. A quiet click of the fingers to set it hunting, one pip of the whistle to stop, two to turn and three to return will have far less disturbing effect on game than continuous shouted orders. When the time comes to retrieve after a shot, the well-trained dog will already be sitting and looking at its handler, so a hand signal to show direction is all that is needed.

Sensible rough shooters also choose their clothes with care. When you want to hide, colour is important, but tone is even more so. A dark country-coloured waxproof shows up almost like a sore thumb against the bleached dead grasses of a marsh in winter; likewise a favourite old pair of moleskins, washed and faded, will seem almost white in the green woods of summer. On the other hand, a grey-brown bunny grazing the green grass of summer is often hardly visible until it runs for cover, because although the colour is different, there is no real tonal contrast with its background.

Think, therefore, about your clothes: a lightweight camouflage coat for summer pigeon shooting, a faded khaki jacket for dry weather wildfowling, and an olive-brown waxproof for the woods in winter. Beware of using camouflage clothing to excess. In today's social climate members of the public can be deeply suspicious of armed and military looking people. If you can get away with using a battered tweed jacket rather than army camouflage gear you will be more likely to be taken for a sportsman rather than a terrorist.

Army camouflage is not always the answer to concealment. Here it sticks out like a sore thumb in the snowy woods of winter. *(John Marchington)*

In the last 10 years a range of much less military camouflage patterns have been imported from across the Atlantic. As well as being less 'confrontational' in public, most are of a better colour and tone than the rather bright 'disruptive pattern material' of the British forces. It is easy to think that you need a different coat for each environment and season, but this is not really so. A dull wetlands or woodland pattern will do for most applications.

Moving stealthily

The lone rough shooter hunting a hedge or patch of wood with his dog obviously needs to flush his game, but he needs to flush it well within shot. Too noisy an approach is apt to have woodcock away at 50 yards and pheasants running on ahead, never to flush. In practice, if he has an efficient dog, the Gun should aim to be as quiet as possible, creeping around the bushes rather than bashing through them. Some care to watch where he puts his feet to avoid the crackle of breaking sticks is also a good idea. In this respect, given dry conditions, a pair of thin-soled shoes may be much better than the traditional wellies, although the modern lightweight green ones are often far more flexible and sensitive than the solid black variety of the past. You can thus feel the sticks underfoot, and avoid putting too much weight on to them.

In certain circumstances the rough shooter will almost need to stalk his quarry, making use of every available kind of cover. A classic case is when a pigeon pitches in a tree 100 yards away. Walk straight in and you have no chance, but if you can choose a biggish tree which is in range of the pigeon, line yourself up with the trunk, and stalk quietly in, a fair offer may be yours.

When to wait

Most of the time the rough shooter will be moving, hunting with his dog and searching for the chance of a shot. Often he will be part of a party, and will have to follow the team lead and walk-up in line or whatever. However, there will be times when he is working alone and when a patient wait may be much more profitable than continued movement. Examples are numerous, but one of the commonest is when pigeons are coming in to roost. The Gun who knows his wood well will often be able to shoot a useful bag by choosing the right area on a stormy afternoon. In flat calm sunny weather, however, a good bag is unlikely, so hunting for bunnies and perhaps the odd wily cock pheasant is much more likely to produce results.

Most wildfowl will leave an area completely if disturbed, but sometimes they will return after a while. This applies particularly to snipe and teal, especially when there are no other suitable pools or boggy patches nearby. Thus, if you flush either of these species on your ramblings, it can pay off to take cover and await their return for 10 or 15 minutes. Similarly a woodcock flushed from an isolated wood is also likely to return after a brief tour of the local countryside having failed to find an alternative covert.

The wise rough shooter begins to learn all about these possibilities, and to

Signs of wigeon in the wet grass. Would you recognise them and know that it meant a chance of an evening flight?

judge when it is worth waiting rather than moving. In the long term his bag is likely to be both heavier and more varied, and therefore much more satisfying.

What's about?

One of the great charms of shooting, and particularly rough shooting, is that there is always the chance of a surprise lurking around the corner. Maybe it is a woodcock in a thick hedge where none has been seen for years, or a gaggle of geese on one of your fields where they have never come before. The rough shooter who keeps his eyes and ears open is far more likely to spot these things and turn them to good account than the chap who cannot see past the end of his gun. Being about early and late is a particular point here. Much of our wildlife is nocturnal or partly so, and it is amazing how few rough shooters stay out until dark. It took me three seasons of evening waits to locate one of the woodcock flightlines described later in this book, but the resultant sport has been well worth it.

Successful rough shooters will also learn to recognise the signs left by the quarry. A pile of droppings under an overgrown hedgerow thorn may indicate the roost site of a lone cock pheasant; and it may be the only one which you will have a chance at for the season if you do not live in a good wild pheasant area and do not release any yourself. Splashes of white guano on the brambles under a clump of pines in your main wood indicate the heart of the pigeon roost area, and hence the place to be with your gun on a stormy winter after-noon. Uprooted grass in the shallows of a wet splash may well be the work of wigeon or teal that you had no idea were visiting your shoot. And so the list goes on.

As you get more familiar with an area you will get better at looking for these signs. One of the most satisfying parts of the game is to predict successfully that, for example, the wigeon ought to be visiting 'Rushy Field' as they usually do in mid-January, if the weather is wet. To then work out a strategy to get onto terms with them, and come home with a couple of truly wild birds as a result of your own study sets the seal on a season's shooting.

2

Quarry Recognition

'To the sportsman-naturalist – and every sportsman should be something of a naturalist if he would derive the full pleasure of his favourite pursuit – there are few more enjoyable occupations than such night watches'

Ed. W. Sandys 'Canoe and Gun' (1897). In Worth Mathewson (ed.) *Wildfowling Tales 1888–1913*. (1989).

Knowing your way around

It goes without saying that it is quite unacceptable behaviour to shoot at anything which has not been positively identified as legal quarry 'in season'. One should therefore never hear the question 'What is it?' when examining the bag – unless from someone other than the Gun responsible for shooting the quarry.

Despite this a surprising number of shooting people lack the basic knowledge of our wildlife, and particularly of birds, which the average bird-watcher would expect of them. In truth this can only detract from their own personal enjoyment of their sport, for half the joy of being out in the countryside is in recognising the wild plants and wildlife which share it with you.

All sportsmen should therefore take nature study seriously. This both ensures that they can always identify their quarry even in the difficult conditions of dawn or evening flight, and means that they will get much more satisfaction out of their sport. The only real way to achieve this is to spend time out in the countryside watching and listening and making full use of whatever opportunities arise to watch wildlife.

Binoculars and field guides

A small pair of pocket binoculars may have a place in the rough shooter's kit-bag, but heavy field guides will not. However, a Sunday morning stroll near

Geese over – but should you shoot? In this case no, they are the fully protected brent.

the local gravel pit or reservoir could teach a lot about wildfowl recognition if you go properly equipped. There are many good field guides on the market.

Regarding binoculars, do not be tempted by too high a magnification. Anything over about 10x is too much when hand held – a tripod is needed for steadiness. The second figure given on a binocular is the objective lens diameter in millimetres: thus 10 × 50 means 10 × magnification and a 50mm objective lens. The larger the objective, the more light gathered and therefore the brighter the image. For portability, the ordinary 8 × 30 has much to recommend it, but serious bird-watchers will probably choose a slightly larger glass at 10 × 50. Real enthusiasts pay several hundred pounds for top-quality roof prism glasses at 10 × 40 or similar specification, but this is probably well beyond the needs of the ordinary rough shooter.

Joining a group
Bird-watching is a tremendously satisfying 'sport' in itself, and joining your local ornithological society on a few of their outings can be a lot of fun. It will also give you an opportunity to learn about other people's attitude to birds, and maybe to defend shooting if you find that some of the members are 'anti'. You may, of course, prefer not to tell them that you shoot – at least to start with – but in practice you are unlikely to make immediate enemies if you do. In the end, it is essential that all shooting people become well versed in all of the conservation issues both for and against their sport, and that they are prepared to defend it in a lucid and scientifically sound manner.

Points to look for
In a brief guide like this, it would be out of place to try and give a detailed account of how to identify each species of quarry and the things with which it might be confused. Some species such as rabbit and pheasant are so familiar to most people that descriptions would be futile anyway.

A pair of gadwall. Wildfowl must be identified with care before taking a shot.

There are, however, specific pointers which are worth bearing in mind. Perhaps the most important is that each species moves in its own way. Thus, when you are decoying pigeon over a stubble, you will watch out for the slightly quicker wing beats of the protected stock dove. Silhouettes vary too – in the case of the stock dove, its tail is proportionately shorter than that of a woodpigeon. Smaller size could also be a help, but is only really useful when you have the two species flying side by side.

Wildfowl are another group where confusion arises easily – especially between the females of the various surface-feeding ducks, all of which are much the same colour. However, movement and silhouette are different, as also is call. The same applies to geese – and these are often very vocal birds. The distinctive 'wink-wink' call of pinkfeet will have the wildfowler's adrenalin pumping long before they come into sight as he waits in his muddy hole at dawn.

In recent times, public attitudes against shooting have hardened. Today it is even more essential that all who shoot are good enthusiastic field naturalists. Arguments suggesting that country people know what is best for the countryside are apt to fall on deaf ears when urban dwellers who use it as a weekend retreat know more about wildlife than many who live there.

For the rough shooter, knowing your birds at first sight, and recognising tracks, trails and signs, gives added confidence in debate. It means that when you argue the rights and wrongs of your sport you are able to move from defence to promotion of the concept of conservation through wise use.

3

The Rough Shooter's Dog

'My gundogs regarded me as a "tail-end Charlie", never "pack leader".'

Chris Cradock *Shooting Times* (25 May 1989)

The need for a dog

The Gun who only fires a shot from a peg or butt on a formal shoot will rarely need a dog. When such events are well organised there should be plenty of pickers-up in the background, and the Gun will rarely have time to pursue a difficult retrieve with his own dog before being called on to the next drive.

The rough shooter, however, very much makes his own sport. When he is decoying pigeons, or stalking rabbits which are grazing, his dog will probably have rather little to do. Sometimes he may even be shooting wildfowl inland

The lone Gun. Rough shooting without a dog is only half a sport. *(The Game Conservancy Trust)*

in a situation where there is no risk of a wounded bird finding water. Generally, however, he will be hunting for his sport, and a good close hunting dog will make an enormous difference to the amount of game which he sees and flushes. Also, he will inevitably either wound the occasional bird or beast or kill one which falls in dense cover or water, in which case an efficient retriever will be essential.

Perhaps more significant still in some ways is the fact that rough shooting is really only half a sport without dogs. They are such an important part of the scene and the pleasure to be had from shooting that anyone who goes forth with his gun but no canine companion is really missing the essence of the sport.

The dog's duties

It is a great mistake to assume that, because rough shooting is less formal than driven, the dogs need to be less well managed. In fact, the reverse is true. A driven game shot with an unsteady dog can easily overcome the problem of running-in. When he arrives at his peg he simply tethers his dog to some firm anchorage such as one of those enormous corkscrew devices which screws into the ground, and forgets it until the drive is over. Not so the rough shooter. The essential difference is that he is almost always on the move and therefore cannot tether his dog, unless to himself, which is dangerous. Also, even if he is happy to have it at heel and on the lead, and does not want to use it to hunt-up his game, he will soon get fed up with its lead tangling in cover.

The rough shooter's dog must be steady.

In practice, the rough shooter's dog should be able to hunt-up and remain well within gunshot (unless it is a pointer) so as not to spoil chances by flushing game too far away. It should then drop or stop to flush, and not chase after either low-flying birds or ground game. Once the gun is fired the dog should remain steady and await further orders, either to carry on hunting if the game was missed, or to find and retrieve whatever was shot. The dog should also be capable of being directed when hunting, and when on the retrieve. It should be possible, too, to handle the dog on to an entirely unseen retrieve, either because it has been unable to mark a fall, or because game shot by another member of the party has not been found.

A Gun's eye view of good dog work. Hunting close in with eyes on the boss for the next order. *(John Marchington)*

Achieving all of this requires training and handling of the highest order, especially when one considers that the Gun will usually only be giving the dog half of his attention, the remainder being on the game and shooting, and the wildlife around him. It is of course well known, that a dog is most likely to riot when you are concentrating least. Temptation is also likely to be greatest at just this time.

Choosing the right dog

The majority of people who read this book will already have a dog, so this section becomes rather academic. However, for anyone about to purchase a new dog, it pays to give some thought to exactly what breed to choose.

Such a decision is apt to cause heated debate amongst field sportsmen, with many strongly held views being passionately argued. In truth, whatever the breed, any well-managed gundog is an asset on a shooting day, and a badly trained one is a nuisance to its owner and everyone else, especially if it interferes with the work of good dogs. There is no doubt, however, that some breeds are better suited to the rough shooter's needs than others.

In most people's minds the first choice is a spaniel, of which the English springer is the most popular. The best spaniels are eternal optimists in even the most barren country, hunting the roughest of cover all day long, remaining close so that game is flushed in shot and retrieving the spoils to hand beautifully. There is no doubt that well-managed spaniels are a joy both to watch and to shoot over. In that sense they are the perfect 'all-round' rough shooter's dog.

The second choice of dogs which have much to offer the rough shooter are the various hunt, point and retrieve breeds, such as German shorthaired pointers, Weimaraner, Visla, Munsterlander and Brittany spaniel. These breeds, like the spaniel, offer both hunting and retrieving skills, and are especially good in more open country such as moorland, rough bracken and bog. The main disadvantage is that a dog coming onto point in thick cover may not be immediately obvious to the handler. He can thus walk on and have game flush behind, and lose a chance of a shot. Also, some of these dogs are apt to avoid rough cover if they get the chance, having learned to quarter open ground in their quest. Nevertheless, those whose sport is mainly in open country may well decide that such a dog is the best bet.

The third choice of likely dogs are the retrievers; Labrador, golden, flatcoat, curly coat and the like. These dogs are bred much more with waiting in mind, at a peg, or in a butt or hide. They are not, therefore, likely to be so well suited as are spaniels to punching through bramble thickets to flush game, although many people succeed in training them to this work very well.

From this it becomes clear that a good, well-trained spaniel is the low ground rough shooter's dog *par excellence*. However, there is no doubt that spaniels, and particularly the best of them, are very demanding dogs to train and handle. If you have the skill, patience and determination you will succeed, but lesser mortals are perhaps better advised to choose an 'easier' option. In this respect, a good steady retriever which has been taught to hunt close in front of its handler has much to recommend it. When the going gets tough, the fact that these dogs are often a little slower than spaniels can be a positive boon in that the handler will find it easier to follow. This does not mean, however, that the handler can afford any lesser degree of control.

A good steady retriever has much to recommend it. (*John Marchington*)

In a sense choice of breed is another facet of the old maxim of choosing 'horses for courses'. One must, however, remember that a very significant part of the course is the temperament of the handler. If you like a particular breed, you will probably do well with it. Beware, however, any tendency to choose because your wife, girlfriend, mother or indeed any other person, likes such and such a breed. If this is the case the wisest decision, unless you are sure that the person concerned understands gundogs, is to be unswayed – or else to buy two pups of different breeds, one of which you *know* will be spoiled.

Another very important point is to ensure that whatever dog you choose comes from working stock. Field trial awards in the pedigree are scoffed at by many people, but at least they are an indication of working ability in a dog's parents – and freedom from such vices as whine and hard mouth. If you do not know the dog's parents intimately, such awards are a good indication that your chosen pup comes from good basic material.

A bunch of the right sort. Always choose good working strains. (*The Game Conservancy Trust*)

Be careful, however, of show blood. In some breeds genuine 'dual purpose' strains do exist; in others you could easily be forgiven for believing that show and working dogs are actually distinct breeds. Perhaps one of the worst examples is the cocker spaniel: the show strains are so highly bred for long ears that the dogs cannot hunt properly without tripping over them or getting them thoroughly tangled in cover. Avoid such monstrosities. If in any doubt, take the advice of an expert who works the breed concerned.

Similarly, be sure to check for any of the congenital or hereditary disorders which afflict your chosen breed. Again, if you are unsure which of the various problems might arise, take the advice of a knowledgeable friend or a veterinary surgeon. Most reputable breeders will, of course, know all about this, and will be at pains to set your mind at rest that they are using good stock.

Caring for your dog

Aside from any legal obligations imposed by cruelty laws, all people who keep dogs are morally obliged to look after them to the best of their ability. Thus, no sportsman will *ever* allow his dog to wander the streets or fields. Apart from the risks of injury or disease, unsupervised exercise leads to self-hunting, for cats, game, poultry or sheep, and once a dog has learned to please itself, it is far less likely to want to please you. Therefore, be sure to house your dog properly when it is not with you.

I kennel my dogs out of doors from the start, as I am firmly convinced that they have better winter coats when they are not allowed to spend their life lying in front of the fire. My neighbours think me hard, but I would be far harder and less caring if I expected an unfit and thin-coated dog to face ice-cold water when shooting in midwinter.

By the same token, feed your dogs well and keep them in what the old-timers called 'hard meat' all year round. A fat dog is an unfit dog, and an unfit dog is more likely to suffer from cold and wet conditions, not to mention the risks of arthritis, heart disease, and kidney failure which so often seem to afflict corpulent dogs before their time.

If your dog, like most, is fed a dry complete diet, remember to weigh or accurately measure its daily ration. If it then starts to get fat, you can easily reduce the amount by a couple of ounces, increasing it again as circumstances dictate. Remember also that healthy dogs do not enjoy their food – they eat so fast that they do not have time to. They just enjoy a full belly. If your dog is not overweight, and it refuses its food, it is almost bound to be unwell, so take this as a warning and be ready to consult the vet unless an obvious reason presents itself. Dry diets are often rather low in fat to avoid deterioration by oxidation. In winter it can pay to add a spoonful of oil to the daily ration to help water-proof the dog's coat.

Responsible dog owners will also ensure that their dogs are regularly inoculated. Apart from being a close friend, your dog is a valuable animal, so do not risk a debilitating or possibly fatal disease.

Training your dog

There are an enormous number of dog training books on the market, mostly written by very experienced people who know far more than I do. It would, therefore, be foolish in the extreme for me to attempt to summarise all this knowledge in a few hundred words with the severe risk that, as a novice, I would get it all wrong anyway. Much better that those who wish to train consult the experts.

Some people are unable to devote the time needed to train a gundog and will

A glove stuffed with socks
makes a good first dummy.
(*The Game Conservancy Trust*)

therefore either buy a pup and send it away, or obtain a 'finished' dog from
a trainer. In either case they will still need to understand gundog psychology
if they are not to ruin the trainer's 18 months hard and expensive work. They
should read a good training manual. In addition, I heartily recommend that
all who handle dogs read and inwardly digest Wilson Stephen's excellent
Gundog Sense and Sensibility (1982).

In most areas of the country there are dog training classes which can be a
great help. Even those people who know how to train a dog can find classes or
group training sessions useful. The distractions and excitement of other people
and their dogs are a real facet of a shooting day, and classes will give a good
simulation of this for the pupil. If you do not know what goes on in your area,
contact the local society for your particular breed, or the Kennel Club itself.

Turning to the actual training, you will, of course, follow the expert advice
and not rush your pupil, nor overdo the length of the lessons and risk boredom.
My paternal grandfather may not have been a dog trainer, but he did have a
useful philosophy of life in his maxim 'Make haste slowly'. Gundog work is
fun, an extension of play, and not just for pups. Dogs are like people, they never
really grow up.

As your puppy grows always bear in mind the basic rules that you should
be absolutely consistent, both in your way of giving orders and in insisting that

Me and my shadow. As a rule, old dogs teach puppies to misbehave, but they can boost the confidence of a diffident pup.

they are carried out. Make sure that each step in the programme is thoroughly fixed in the dog's mind before you move on to the next. And, do not try out anything new unless you are confident that it will work – and have decided what to do if it does not. If your dog fails, look to yourself for the reason. It is almost bound to be a case of confusion because of a mistake on your part. This does not mean that you should ignore disobedience; if the dog knows what you mean when giving an order you must be prepared to enforce it.

As mentioned earlier, steadiness to flush and shot is essential in a rough shooting dog, so do not make the mistake of allowing it to run-in, believing that it will be possible to correct this later. Teach your dog to sit and stay, and to drop to the stop whistle wherever it is. In this way you will always have control when it is needed without the disturbance of needing to shout orders. You will then find it easy to train the dog to take hand signals. Most of the time you will not need to use these skills, as a well-trained dog almost automatically does the right things, but when you need hand signals you probably need them badly, so do not skimp on the job.

Initiative on the part of the dog is so valuable that you should not crush it. Therefore, for example, when it is working in the right general area hunting or retrieving, do not interfere. Much better, leave it to its own devices until it looks to you for help. This will be particularly important when working at evening flight, when you may have even less idea than the dog of where to look. Training in the dark in the later stages will help to teach a puppy to mark by hearing – a very valuable talent if fowling is part of your sport.

The finished partnership between man and dog is immensely satisfying. It is also an ongoing relationship which requires constant attention. Old dogs can learn to disobey just as easily as young ones, so do not relax too much or you may receive a serious shock. This is most likely to happen during the close season, when work is a distant thought, and you are taking an evening stroll and not really concentrating on your dog.

4

Guns and Cartridges

'I always swore by size 6 shot. But much water has passed under the cartridge-making bridge . . . I now almost exclusively use 7s . . .'

Archie Coats *Pigeon Shooting* 2nd Edition (1970).

'Fours for duck, 1s for geese and 5s or 6s for pheasant' – What is the best shot size to use? This question causes more heated arguments than any other in shooting. Anyone who is undecided for himself will hear so many differing opinions and so many sincerely held viewpoints that only confusion will reign. Before deciding which size to use it is perhaps best to consider how a gun works.

The shotgun and how it works

It may be stating the obvious, but it is nevertheless vital to understand that a shotgun has a smooth bore. When you fire your gun you are sending a hail of shot, and *not* a single carefully aimed projectile. Thus, no matter how good a shot you are, you can only centre your pattern on the target and hope that some of the pellets strike. A bird-shaped hole right in the centre of the pattern is not entirely beyond the realms of possibility, and may well be invoked by some Guns as the reason for a miss!

Shotguns are widely held to kill by a combination of shock, due to many pellets striking, and the effect of blows by individual pellets on vital organs. Some of the older texts on shooting even give values for the necessary striking energy of individual pellets for various quarry species. This does, however, beg a serious question – namely whether an equally powerful blow to different vital organs has the same effect. Study of rifle shooting suggests that this is not so. For example, it is a fact that silenced .22 rifles are widely used by poachers to shoot deer even though this calibre is well below the legal minimum

The rifle user knows that shots into the heart or lungs may not cause instant death. *(The Game Conservancy Trust)*

allowed. However, a clean kill is only likely to result if the tiny .22 bullet hits the vertebrae of the neck. A much more powerful weapon is considered necessary for a shot into the heart/lung area. Even this may not result in instant collapse, with the beast often running on for some distance before falling. To take our example one stage further, a shot in the belly with an elephant rifle will not stop the deer at all. The beast may well bleed to death, but it could also simply starve over a period of several days, despite the enormous shock which must occur at the impact of such a bullet.

My own observations of the effects of a shotgun lead me to similar conclusions. No amount of shots in the belly, no matter how large, will bring your bird down. Being mainly a wildfowler and rough shooter has allowed me to examine my own bag when plucking and dressing for the oven in a way which most driven shooters never achieve. A striking example of what can happen is given by a September mallard, a couple of seasons ago. This particular bird was high and fell quite dead on the mudflats. When plucked there was not a blemish, so I skinned the head and neck to find that a single pellet had hit the upper neck and killed the bird outright. The reverse case is illustrated by another mallard: one of a pair, both of which were shot; this bird staggered in the air and then flew on for over 200 yards before planing down into the water, where it died almost immediately. It carried a total of 14 hits; 3 in the wing muscles (but not the bones) and 11 in the body. Two pellets had passed right through, one had pierced the heart and two the lungs. There was not a single

This Canada goose fell with a broken wing and needed its neck wrung, despite having some pellets pass right through its body.

pellet in the head, neck or spine. Thus, just like a heart-shot deer, this bird had flown on before collapse – quite far enough to have made it impossible to retrieve in many circumstances.

The clear message that comes from all of this is that the 'real target' on our quarry is confined to the head and upper spine. Anything else is unlikely to bring the bird down close enough for it to be gathered easily, except a broken wing and this alone is clearly unsatisfactory.

One pellet right through the lungs. This bird flew 300 yards before collapse.

Suitable cartridges

During my apprenticeship to wildfowling, my father insisted on smaller shot than many authors have recommended, and we always used No. 6 shot. I started with Eley's famous Impax loads with 28g (1oz) of shot, and graduated to Hymax at 36g (1¼oz). An experiment with 5s proved unsatisfactory. It's true that the odd long shot came off, but far too many birds fell wounded rather than dead. And 4s were even more erratic.

About ten seasons ago, having gone back to Grand Prix 6s, I ran out of this size, but found I had a case of Impax 7s which I generally reserved for woodcock. To my surprise, I found that they worked admirably. I still missed with much the same frequency, but the proportion of wounded birds fell dramatically.

Today, for all normal game shooting and wildfowling purposes, I use these 28g (1oz) loads of 7s, with my gun bored improved cylinder in both barrels. If I were marksman enough to use full choke reliably, I might go up to 6s for extra range, but I know that my shooting would deteriorate dramatically.

Geese pose a special problem, for they so often go by at extreme range, and everyone is searching for the ideal combination of pattern density and striking energy. Even here, I break with tradition and use 4s or 5s rather than 3s. Recently I was surprised by a Canada coming in from behind. I took a hurried shot and it fell very dead to a 28g (1oz) load of 7s from quite a reasonable altitude.

When one considers how small a target area the bones of the head and neck present, it becomes clear that one of the easiest ways to fell a high goose is to break a wing, since the wing bones actually form a larger target. I think that there is a severe risk that one tries, if quite subconsciously, for a broken wing at high flying geese when stepping up the shot size. The trouble is that if the bird falls and is retrieved, it is easy to forget that it needed dispatching when

One pellet in the head killed this teal outright. Note the tiny target presented by head and neck – much smaller than a clay pigeon.

it came to hand. Also, for every bird that falls, either dead or winged, there will be others which are also hit in the body with pellets which have enough energy to bury deep into the internal organs where they can result in a slow and painful death. If one is tempted by an over-long shot with smaller pellets, however, they are likely only to penetrate just under the skin. This is bad enough, but at least there is a good chance that the bird will survive with little or no long-term effect.

My own system, therefore, is to use open bores and small shot which give a high chance of hits to head and neck and subsequent clean kills. At the same time one has to learn the essential restraint *not to shoot at birds at the limit of range or beyond*. By this I mean about 35 metres.

At the other end of the size scale come snipe. These are such a small quarry that 7's really are a little large. My best successes over the years have been with 8's, and I would use skeet loads of 9's rather than 7's if I could not obtain 8's.

Non-toxic loads

The question of poisoning of waterfowl through ingestion of spent lead shot has come to the fore in the last few years. In England and Wales it is now a legal requirement to use a non-toxic alternative for all wildfowl shooting, plus coot and moorhen. Lead is also banned on the foreshore and on a long list of Sites of Special Scientific Interest (SSSIs).

In Scotland it is illegal to use lead over all wetlands, whatever the quarry. Meanwhile, the code of good shooting practice says that lead should not be used, even for game shooting, where there is a risk that it will fall on wetlands of significance to feeding waterfowl.

Various alternatives are on offer, and some materials have come and gone. The commonest at present are as follows:

- *Steel* – The cheapest alternative, steel shot is in fact made from short lengths of soft iron wire which are mechanically rounded. It has two main drawbacks. First, the density is much lower than lead so it needs to be pushed harder by the powder charge to maintain effectiveness. Secondly, it is much harder than lead, which means that it could scratch your barrels. This problem is overcome by using heavy cup wads so that the shot does not come into contact with the bore. However, the hard nature also brings a risk of ring bulges to barrels – steel should *never* be used in barrels tighter than half choke. To overcome the lighter weight of the shot, the standard advice is to use *two* sizes larger than you would for lead. My own experience, mostly with steel 5s in place of my normal lead 7s, is that any reduction in performance is not as serious as many have made out. My biggest objection is not that steel does not kill, but that I do not like hard lumps of iron on the dinner plate. I suspect that dentists will love the stuff! I should add that steel loads are not suitable for use in old damascus-barrelled guns. As with any other cartridge, be sure that your gun is proved to take it.

- *Bismuth* – More expensive than steel, but only a little less dense than lead. The density is so similar that the standard advice is to stick to the same shot size as you would for lead. Bismuth is available in all the normal loads down to size 7. There is some worry that big shot sizes in heavy loads for big-bore wildfowling guns may tend to break up, but this is unlikely to affect the rough shooter. My own experience is that this substitute works fine. After several seasons of regular use I detect no significant difference from lead.
- *Tungsten matrix* – More expensive again, and virtually the same density as lead. Although tungsten itself is very hard, the matrix mix is quite soft. There is a little worry that the tungsten powder in the matrix might polish the bore and cause some extra wear compared to lead, but the normal loads are in cup wads which would prevent this anyway. Tungsten matrix seems to react rather oddly to choke, with tightly choked guns producing bad or 'blown' patterns. However, in normal borings there is no sign of problems. Tungsten is available down to U.S. shot size 6 (our No. 5), so those who prefer small shot are not catered for. My own experience is limited, but I have used quite a few size 5 loads (our size 4) on geese and mallard and found them the equal of lead.
- *Tungsten alloys* – Tungsten itself is much denser than lead, very expensive and very hard. It has recently become available in alloys of which 'Hevi-shot' is the most well known. This is a little denser than lead, and very hard. Like steel it needs to be used in cup wads and may cause trouble if fired through tight chokes.

In conclusion, having used all the alternatives, I have come to bismuth as my choice for most purposes, but I stress again that hard lumps in my dinner is the main reason for not using steel. For geese I am just as happy with tungsten matrix. My biggest objection (other than cost) is at the other end of the size scale where there is no really suitable shot for snipe. I make do with bismuth 7s where lead is illegal, but I really do not shoot them with the same confidence or effectiveness as the lead 8s, which have always been my favourite for these tiny but delicious birds.

Suitable guns

Having decided that an ordinary game load of small shot suits most of our requirements, most of the time, we come to the decision of what gun to use. Most readers will probably own a gun anyway, in which case the exact choice of weapon becomes rather an academic question. However, guns can be adapted in many ways, and adaptations may improve performance.

For most men a 12-bore will be the probable choice, although ladies may well choose a slightly lighter gun, and the 20-bore has much to recommend it. Indeed, many men having lugged a 12-bore around for some years revert to the 20 to reduce the weight which they have to carry. Going too far down the

The classic game gun – a double side by side twelve bore. *(The Game Conservancy Trust)*

weight reduction road does have drawbacks, however, for light guns can recoil badly if used with too heavy a load. There is an age-old formula which says that recoil becomes a noticeable problem if there is less than 6lb of gun for each ounce of shot fired (or in metric terms 100g for every gram fired). Thus, it is easy for the father buying a small gun for his son to make the mistake of imposing excessive recoil by choosing too light a weapon. Most 12-bore game guns weigh between 2.9kg (6½lb) and 3.2kg (7lb) and are ideally suited to the standard 30g (1 $^{1}/_{16}$oz) load. Provided they are proved to take it, they will fire the odd 36g (1¼oz) wildfowling load if you want it, but most people will not find such a gun too heavy to carry all day.

If you choose a 20-bore for whatever reason, beware of any gun weighing less than about 2.5kg (5½lb) as many modern 20-bore cartridges carry 26g ($^{7}/_{8}$oz) of shot and could kick like the proverbial mule if used in a lighter gun. This may not matter to the experienced shot, but could be very uncomfortable for a newcomer to shooting.

A single-barrelled gun has much to recommend it, not least that it teaches you to make best use of your offers. If you miss first barrel there is no second chance. However, most people will choose a double to give them that extra chance. A semi-automatic can do the same job, but does have some drawbacks. First, with a few minor exceptions, it is illegal to use a semi-automatic with a magazine capable of holding more than two shots against birds, so a five-shot is only suitable for rabbits and hares. The five-shot, whether semi-auto or pump also now requires a part 1 firearm certificate following the Firearms (Amendment) Act, (1988). Aside from these legal difficulties, both types are rather slower to load and unload. This becomes a particular aggravation when there are lots of fences to cross. There can be a strong temptation not to unload when crossing obstacles. *Don't be tempted.* The dangers are enormous, even when you are alone.

Assuming that you have concluded that a double-barrelled 12-bore or 20-bore shotgun is the best choice for you, you have still to decide between two barrel configurations. The more traditional form of double is the side-by-side (s/s) in which the barrels lie alongside each other. In the over-and-under (o/u) type they lie one above the other. There are still a few 'posher' and more formal shoots where the o/u configuration is frowned upon as cheap and foreign (unless of course, it is a pair of best English guns built by Boss or Purdey in the 1930s). All this need not bother the rough shooter – he can make a choice based on other considerations, and either form will do admirably for his purpose.

The o/u is generally favoured by clay shooters, who claim that the narrower sight plane from looking down a single barrel aids accuracy. Also, most o/u guns are a little heavier than s/s guns which helps to absorb recoil and ease the strain of firing lots of shots. Lastly, the bottom barrel of the o/u is normally fired first. Being lower down this is nearer to being in line with the shoulder than either barrel on an s/s, so there is less 'muzzle flip', which means that you can get back on to your target more quickly for a second shot if you miss.

The s/s configuration has the advantage of a lighter average weight (if you want it), and a shorter drop when you break and open. This latter means that

Over and Under guns are increasingly popular, and ideal in most respects for the rough shooter. *(Ian Grindy)*

you are less likely to block the muzzles with soil when reloading, and also that you need a little less room to operate in a pigeon or duck hide. This can be a serious consideration when you are in an exposed situation and need the smallest hide to remain unobtrusive.

Having decided upon what you fancy, you now come to a much more serious question – gunfitting. Shotguns are not aimed like a rifle, but pointed. Thus, when the gun is mounted in your shoulder it must point *exactly* where you are looking if the charge is to end up on target. Guns which are too long, too short, too low in the comb, or wrong in one of the many other subtle ways which a good gunsmith or shooting coach understands are all too common. Since everyone is slightly different from his neighbour, everyone requires a slightly different gun stock. Guns can, usually, be relatively easily adjusted, and the frustration of missing or wounding game which you should have killed more than justifies the small cost. So go to a competent expert and take advice.

While your gun is being adjusted, consider how much choke you need. I am not a great shot and therefore know that I need the widest spread possible to allow me to do well. The best thing which I ever did for my shooting – and particularly at high birds, was having my chokes opened out to improved cylinder. As mentioned earlier I find open boring and 28g (1oz) loads of No. 7 shot ideal for almost all of my shooting.

Proof

If you are going out to buy a second-hand gun it is best to buy from a reputable dealer. This may involve a little more expense than buying on the open market, but at least you know that the dealer must be satisfied that the gun is safe and in proof. The law requires that all guns which are sold must pass a proof test to ensure that they are not liable to blow up in use. This involves deliberately overloading them under test in a proof house. The gun is then marked with a chamber length and a service pressure. Be sure that all the cartridges which you use in your gun fall within these proof standards.

Worn or abused guns may well still bear proof marks but fall below the correct standards. If you wish to buy a gun privately, and do not understand either proof or what to look for regarding the signs of wear or neglect, consult someone who does, and be sure to have the gun checked by a gunsmith before you use it.

Gun care and cleaning

Guns are made from metals which are very prone to corrosion, and should always be carefully cleaned after use. Put a wet gun into its sleeve for the two-hour journey home after a day in the rain, and you will probably find it covered in rust spots when you arrive. Always wipe it dry and apply fresh oil as soon after use as possible. I usually do this when I get back to the car.

The gun is then carefully cleaned when I get home. To do this I remove the forend and break it down into its three main parts. The barrels are mopped through and oiled inside and out, and the other metal parts carefully but lightly oiled. Take care not to overdo this. Gun oils rot wood, and a heavily oiled gun left standing up in a cabinet is liable to drain oil down into the area where stock and action are joined, eventually leading to loosening of the stock. It is probably best to store your gun barrels down to help eliminate this problem.

By the same token, care should be taken not to get gun oil on to wooden parts. In this respect, aerosol oils are a particular risk. While they often act as good moisture repellents, they tend to drive oil onto or even into the wood. Careful application with an oily rag or brush may be more time consuming, but it is also more precise.

All guns should be opened up annually to examine for possible deterioration. This is a job for a skilled gunsmith, so unless you are fully conversant with what to do, do not do it yourself. Remember, you would not expect your car to start first time for ever without regular servicing. The same applies to guns, and the frustration of a needless breakdown when out shooting is immense, not to mention the safety risks of long-term neglect.

Safe gun handling

Always treat your gun as if it were loaded. That way you should never get into the habit of doing anything which may be dangerous. It is really outside the remit of this book to go into minute detail regarding shooting, marks-

Always look down the bores before you load up. A blocked barrel can lead to your gun blowing up.

manship, and safety. Anyone who is completely new to shooting should take lessons from a professional, or join a gun club and break a few clays under guidance. They should also get a good book on guns, shooting and safety.

Shooting has an enormous number of unwritten conventions about what is considered acceptable behaviour, and most of them have a safety aspect built in. Shooting at very low birds is a good example. This is considered unsportsmanlike because such shots are often easy and the game is often ruined for the table because it is too close. It is also downright dangerous in company, since someone who swings on a low bird is likely to end up pointing his gun at someone else. On the other hand, a pigeon or duck dead low but well out over the decoys may be a very fair and worthwhile shot for the lone gunner who can see clearly that there is no one nearby.

Do remember that you do *not* need to point directly at someone to shoot them. Pellets spread in a cone from a shotgun, and odd pellets that go off at a tangent are not uncommon. These 'fliers' have been known to go out at 30° from the point of aim, so the accepted etiquette is never to bring your muzzles to an angle of closer than 45° to anyone.

5

Clothes and Equipment

'Any fool can be uncomfortable.'

Robin Bucknall

Staying warm, dry and comfortable

The full sense of my chum Robin's witty maxim for life took some time to sink in. Fools *may* be uncomfortable . . . but the rest of us should strive to avoid this. Shooting should bring enormous pleasure to its participants, in which case discomfort cannot fit into any logical design for the sport. Even the coastal wildfowler, who is reputed to face the most uncomfortable of sporting lives, rarely gets his feathers seriously ruffled if he goes to the shore well prepared.

Being suitably clad for all events requires considerable thought for the rough shooter. He may, at various times of year face anything from a scorching July afternoon walking at the hedgerows for pigeons and rabbits, to a cold pre-dawn vigil in January snows waiting for duck or geese to flight. Each trip out with the gun needs a little forethought, and also an ear to the weather forecast, to ensure a comfortable choice of clothing. However, the rough shooter is usually more active than passive, in which case the likeliest mistake is to wear too much and work up a sweat. Even on a frosty day, the Gun on the move is likely to find a shirt, a thin jumper and a tweed or breathable jacket provide plenty of insulation. On the other hand, if he then intends to wait by a pool at evening flight, his game-bag should contain a thick jersey, a hat and perhaps a pair of fingerless gloves. In this way he will ensure that he is not frozen to the marrow, and thus slow and clumsy to mount his gun, when the teal finally come fizzing in offering only a fleeting chance in the last light.

The most important item on the list of kit for general use is undoubtedly a fully waterproof coat. A few years ago I would have selected waxed cotton as the only really practical choice, but today things are different. Goretex has made enormous inroads into the market for outdoor coats and is still gaining in popularity, despite its comparatively high price. Other breathable fabrics have made their mark too; milair is particularly good. There is a bewildering array of outer shell materials, for most of these coats simply have a waterproof drop liner and then whatever inner lining the manufacturer thinks best. For cold weather a good tough tweed outer layer and a warm lining are ideal, but much lighter alternatives are also available. Be aware also that tweed, although comfortable, absorbs a lot of water in wet weather, and can be very heavy. Choice of colour is wide too, and most breathable shooting coats are less obtrusive than the standard, rather dark waxproof. This issue and its relevance to camouflage is discussed in greater detail in Chapter 1.

When choosing a waterproof of whatever type, try to find one which is a little longer than average. In this way you will be able to use leggings rather than overtrousers in wet weather without suffering a damp backside. In this respect I still feel that stud-on waxproofs are hard to beat. I carry a pair of these folded small along with a belt to support them, in my game-bag unless I am sure that it is going to be a completely dry day, with no patches of dripping dew-soaked kale to be walked up.

For footwear I choose leather boots every time if it is going to be dry enough, much preferring these to wellies. However, when the going is wet, wellies are essential. In which case I advise against the practice of buying the cheapest. Do

Face masks help to hide the most obvious part of you, but many shooters find them uncomfortable. *(The Game Conservancy Trust)*

yourself and your feet a favour and get a comfortable pair. I find neoprene-lined ones the best. The soles are a little more forgiving than most, your feet stay warm, and I do not find them over hot even in summer. However, if you run to more than one pair, then lightweight ones are a good second set. What I do suggest, is to find a pair that are a good fit to your calves. The old heavy black rubber sort that wobble around on your legs are uncomfortable. They are also very noisy when you are trying to creep up on something.

At the opposite end of the body, given dry weather, I rarely bother with a hat when on the move. However, I keep a hood fitted to my jacket in case of a wet wait at flight time. For cold dry weather I prefer a plain woolly hat without a brim, choosing a tweed hat with a peak fore and aft when it turns wet. This latter helps keep the rain out of the eyes and sheds it past the collar at the back – not down the neck. However, a brim on your hat forces you to turn more of your horribly pale face towards your quarry when waiting for ducks, geese or pigeons at flight. You should, of course, always try to arrange things so that you are looking through a thin veil of cover in these circumstances, but even so, a wide brim is often a hindrance and not a help.

In really cold weather some form of protection for the hands may be needed, but I try to avoid this until it is really essential. Cold hands are really an early indication of a cold body, so an extra thermal vest may be the best answer. I find considerable difficulty in shooting in gloves, but do use the fingerless type when it is really cold. Woollen or thermal ones are fine when it is dry, but if soaked by rain or sleet they are no help at all. For these conditions I use a pair of waterproof gloves with thermal lined plastic backs and soft leather palms. (These came with just the trigger finger cut off, though still too much left on. However, it was easy to shorten and remove the rest.)

Having kept the wind and rain out, what you choose to wear under all of this is obviously up to you. However, I do recommend breeks and stockings as they are more comfortable than trousers tucked into socks when stuffed into wellies. Also, a thermal waistcoat has much to recommend it in cold weather in that it helps to keep the shoulders and lower back warm without interfering with arm movement. As mentioned earlier, however, beware too much clothing. If you are on the move you will probably stay warm anyway. Also, if you have a strenuous walk to morning flight or a pigeon hide, it is wise to carry spare clothing in your bag. You then walk out in minimum clothing and add the extras when you get into position. The alternative is to put the lot on, work up a dreadful sweat as you struggle out across the marsh or ploughed fields, and then get very cold very quickly once you stand or sit still.

Hearing protection

When I started shooting, about 40 years ago, the damage that gunfire can do to your hearing was poorly recognised. Today, in my mid-forties, I am remarkably lucky. After all that shooting, mostly without hearing protection, I still hear fairly well. But the damage is done. I have serious trouble picking up individual conversations in a noisy pub and there are other symptoms too.

I wish I had been more careful over the last 30 years. More importantly, I hope that young shooters will learn from the mistakes made by older generations. Please take hearing protection very seriously. Also, remember that the damage is progressive. The more you shoot the worse it gets. So even if you have lost some hearing already it is not too late to stop the rot.

For clay shoots and driven days simple earmuffs are fine and very effective, but for the rest of your sport you will probably want to hear both conversation and wildlife. Electronic ear muffs, valve ear plugs, or even electronic ear plugs, are all available. With varying efficiency they all allow you to hear normal sounds but cut out loud noises. They all cost money, but what price do you put on hearing the dawn chorus in your dotage?

Safety glasses

Many cartridge boxes carry a safety warning that includes eye protection on its list of recommendations. In practice most shooters do not bother. However, shooting does result in things falling out of the sky; fragments of branches, broken clays, bits of wadding and even the odd dead bird. Any of them can fall in your eye and at the very least spoil your day. The best shooter's safety specs can even take a direct hit from a pellet at quite close range, so they could save your eyesight in the event of a shooting accident.

Game-bags and cartridge belts

I am continually amazed at the number of shooters who turn out for a walked-up day with no means of carrying spoils. Even a few snipe in the jacket pockets can pull on your shoulders and impair your gunmounting or swing, and a hare in the hand is a positive encumbrance. I suppose that some people carry no bag in the hope that a fellow Gun will offer to carry their game. Well, I have given up doing this. If you shoot a hare when out with me I might offer to *rent* you my bag provided that you act as my bearer if I shoot something as well.

For most purposes, an ordinary small game-bag, with its net front is ideal. It will hold three or four birds the size of a pheasant and the better part of a dozen pigeons, as well as a spare box of cartridges or a thermos flask if needed, and a pair of neatly folded leggings in case things get wet. If I expect to have to carry more than this, perhaps for a day at pigeons, I also have a very large game-bag. Many folk have poked fun at this, but at least it makes a comfortable way to carry a heavy load. The net fitted on the front of most game-bags has plus and minus points. It does help game to cool quickly, maintaining better table quality. However, it can have a nasty habit of catching on brambles, briars and barbed wire – the last of which is particularly annoying – and cannot be extracted by brute force. Also, it does advertise your success to passers-by, and dead wildlife on view can be offensive to some folk. Lastly, the netting has a habit of rotting and breaking after a few years – do not make the mistake made by one eminent sportsman of my acquaintance who lost his entire day's bag of one teal when walking home after dark. Hanging your bag up to dry properly after a wet day helps to prolong the life of the net.

A backpack is easier to carry and less inclined to swing around and throw you off balance than a bag slung across the shoulder and hanging to one side, making it easier to cross fences, ditches and other obstacles. However, such an arrangement is an awful aggravation if it has to be unslung every time you shoot something when walking-up over productive ground. I therefore choose an ordinary game-bag for the latter type of sport and a backpack of suitable size when I have a longish walk to and from a static flighting position.

There are 'posh' shoots where a cartridge belt is definitely frowned upon. I suppose that the implication is either that the contents of the belt are bound to be inadequate, or that gentlemen always have a bearer to deal with that sort of thing. For the rough shooter the practicalities of a belt far outweigh any such social considerations. The weight distribution is comfortable and a beltful should cover all but red-letter days. Also, if like me you have a conscience about plastic litter, you will use paper cased cartridges with biodegradable fibre or felt wads. Hopefully, you will not leave spent cases anyway, but if in the heat of the moment you do drop one a paper case will rot away. With a belt underneath your waterproof coat you are in an even better position than your forefathers to keep your powder bone dry in even the wettest conditions. A few more cartridges in your pockets, and a cartridge extractor on a string around your neck, and you should be able to cope with all eventualities.

Knives, calls and other gadgets

A pocket knife covers a multitude of potential problems from field dressing of game to minor running repairs to your gun should a breakdown occur. A surprising number of countrymen fail to carry one nevertheless – do not be one of them. Today's easy-care age means that most knives have a stainless blade, which is a pity. Good quality high-carbon steel may have needed a little more care, but it was much easier to sharpen and usually held a much better edge. The French Opinel knives employ a quite good grade of steel, have a blade lock to avoid accidental closure on your fingers, and are comfortable to work with. Far too many knives bristle with unnecessary gadgets which only serve to blister your hands when you have some serious cutting to do. Always keep your knife sharp. Blunt knives are dangerous – you have to push harder and when you slip an accident is almost bound to occur.

A spent cartridge jammed into the chamber is not confined to paper cases, so a small cartridge extractor is valuable to all. I carry mine on a lanyard slung round my neck to which calls and compass can be attached. The latter is really only a hill walker's or coastal fowler's tool, and so outside the scope of this book.

Another handy item which weighs nothing and occupies no space, is a piece of rag. Guns are apt to slip in muddy hands, so the rag is useful for this and to wipe your gun if you get it dirty. Do not forget that mud on the outside soon gets into the works, but if you wipe it off to start with the problem does not arise.

If you do not feel confident to humanely dispatch any wounded game by stretching its neck, carry a priest or a pair of dispatch pliers. The latter simply sever the spine with a quick squeeze and are very efficient.

Calling is a much under-practised art in the United Kingdom compared with the New World. A well-blown call can add enormously to your success when flighting wildfowl, especially at dawn or dusk, or in poor light conditions. Single ducks and geese are particularly susceptible. However, calling is a great art, and it is easy to blow a wrong note and spoil a good chance at the last minute. Indeed, on a flight pool, it is odds on that circling ducks will come anyway, if you do not scare them off by showing yourself or shooting too soon. However, in more open circumstances on the water meadows or stubbles, duck may be attracted into shot when they start circling some distance away. As a general rule, do not blow the call too often, and stop if they are coming well anyway. It is far too easy to blow a raspberry and scare them away. The Olt 66 mallard call has proved particularly successful for me.

A wigeon whistle can be remarkably successful too, and most folk can learn to imitate their call quite well without buying a fancy call. In my own wildfowling apprenticeship I learned wigeon and curlew, which means that half my repertoire is now redundant, since curlew became protected in 1981.

Geese also respond to a call well, and pinkfeet do so particularly. In my experience greylags are less responsive, but seem to decoy well anyway. I have little experience of whitefronts, and am unable to comment, but find that

Dispatch pliers are an efficient method of killing wounded birds.

singles or small groups of Canadas come quite well too. I therefore carry an Olt model L-22 goose call when a chance of geese is on. Blown as instructed this gives a very good Canada call, which is what its American manufacturers designed it for. Fortuitously, it imitates the 'wink-wink' of a pinkfoot remarkably well if blown *hard* twice in rapid succession. My friend Arthur Cannon of Lancashire, with whom I have spent several enchanting dawn flights, uses a squeaker salvaged from a Christmas 'blowout'. It does not have the volume of a commercial call, but the note is as near a perfect imitation of a pinkfoot as I have heard. However, all brands do not have the same note, so you could well have some fun stealing them from the kids' Christmas crackers and trying to find the right one.

Commercial wood pigeon calls are available too, though I must confess that I have only tried one once. It did not do me any good – I suspect that it is only really effective for odd birds at breeding time. Pigeons are not social callers, they call to attract a mate and keep a breeding territory.

Decoys are such an important part of the shooter's art that they and their use deserve a chapter to themselves (see Chapter 14).

6

Legal and Ethical Considerations

'Never, never let your gun pointed be at anyone.'

Mark Beaufoy *A Father's Advice* (1903)

Fieldsportsmen are under increasing public scrutiny in every way. Against this background, it is essential that everyone who carries a gun has a comprehensive understanding of the law as it affects country sports and conservation in general. In a book such as this it is only possible to give a brief account of some of the more significant legislation.

The Bibliography includes publications covering various aspects of the law in relation to shooting, but I take this opportunity of recommending Charlie Parkes and John Thornley's excellent and comprehensive work *Fair Game: The Law of Country Sports and the Protection of Wildlife* (2000) and David Frost's *Sporting Firearms and the Law* (1997). Both are essential reading for all rough shooters.

Possession of guns

The Firearms (Amendment) Act 1988 has considerably tightened controls over the possession of shotguns. With very few exceptions, anyone who has a shotgun in his possession (whether owned, hired or simply on loan) needs to hold a shotgun certificate issued by the Chief Constable of Police for the area in which he normally resides. Contrary to popular belief, there is no lower age limit on holding a shotgun certificate, so you can apply at the local police station for a shotgun certificate for your son or daughter at whatever age you consider they should start shooting.

There is also no requirement to have a place to shoot, but you do have to show a good reason for wishing to own a gun. Accepting invitations to shoot from friends, even though you have no ground of your own, is normally adequate. The Chief Constable does, however, have the right to refuse a certificate to anyone who has been sentenced to certain forms of imprisonment or who he considers is a danger to the peace. Persons under the age of 15 may not use, nor have an assembled gun in their possession, unless either supervised by someone aged 21 or over, or secured in a gun cover so that it may not be fired. Between 15 and 17 years of age it is legal to use a shotgun unsupervised, but not to buy one or to buy cartridges. Even those above the age of 17 will need to show their shotgun certificate when buying either a gun or cartridges. The certificate also requires a list of all guns in your possession but there is no restriction on how many you may own.

The 1988 Act also imposes a statutory requirement for shotgun owners to keep their weapons in a secure place with a view to preventing, so far as is reasonably practicable, access to them by unauthorised persons. A 'secure place' and 'reasonably practicable' are not defined, and different constabularies have different interpretations. In practice most gun owners will value their weapons highly enough to wish to lock them away when not in use, and many people now have metal security cabinets. In many senses, hiding the weapons from the view of the casual thief is more important. Also, it is a wise policy to hide a key component, such as the forend, in a different place, thus effectively de-activating the gun if it is stolen.

Repeating and semi-automatic guns

With minor exceptions, The Wildlife and Countryside Act, 1981 prohibits the use of semi-automatic guns (that is, those which reload automatically each time they are fired) with a magazine capable of holding more than two cartridges against birds. This effectively reduces the weapon to three shots (two in the magazine and one in the chamber). Pump actions with larger magazines are not affected since they are loaded manually between each shot.

However, both types of gun are scheduled as Section 1 firearms by the Firearms (Amendment) Act, 1988, unless they meet the official criterion of having a magazine capable of holding not more than two cartridges. This therefore makes them a less than practical proposition for the all round rough shooter.

Rights to shoot

Anyone who takes a gun of any kind, including an airgun, on to land where they do not have lawful authority, or reasonable excuse to do so, commits the criminal offence of armed trespass (Firearms Act, 1968). If they then proceed to shoot, or attempt to shoot, any game the further offence of poaching is added. The game and poaching laws are extremely complex, and in many senses archaic, with some offences considered far more serious than others. The rough shooter hardly need worry greatly about all of this, provided that he does have permission to shoot on the ground he uses. Being tempted to stray over your

American teal, a rare visitor to Britain, and fully protected by the Wildlife and Countryside Act, 1981.

boundaries could lead to loss of access to your land, and of your certificate and gun. Those who wish to know more are again referred to *Fair Game: The Law of Country Sports and the Protection of Wildlife* mentioned earlier and which gives a very full account.

Please also remember to be clear about what you can do on your shoot. Shooting leases vary according to the requirements of the landlord. Read yours carefully and make sure that you comply with it. Also, if you simply have verbal permission to shoot on the land concerned, be sure not to exceed what your host has kindly allowed you to do. If you have been given permission to shoot the pigeons on the peas on a certain field, stay there and only shoot pigeons.

Quarry lists and open seasons
The list of what the British rough shooter can shoot is controlled by a number of different Acts of Parliament. The two most important are The Game Act, 1831 (Game [Scotland] Act, 1832) and The Wildlife and Countryside Act, 1981. The former covers a selection of gamebirds, and the latter covers all other quarry birds. The open seasons are as follows (dates inclusive).

Grouse	12 August – 10 December
Ptarmigan (Scotland only)	12 August – 10 December
Blackgame	20 August – 10 December
Partridge (redleg and grey)	1 September – 1 February
Pheasant	1 October – 1 February
Snipe	12 August – 31 January
Woodcock (England and Wales)	1 October – 31 January

Woodcock (Scotland)	1 September – 31 January

Coot	
Moorhen	1 September – 31 January
Golden Plover	

Greylag goose	
Pinkfooted goose	
Canada goose	
Whitefronted goose (England and Wales only)	
Mallard	1 September – 31 January except in or over areas below high water mark of ordinary spring tides, where the season extends to 20 February.
Teal	
Pintail	
Wigeon	
Gadwall	
Shoveller	
Tufted duck	
Pochard	
Goldeneye	

There is also a list of 'pest' birds which may be shot (or cage trapped) all the year round as a result of a series of open general licences issued by the Department of the Environment, Food and Rural Affairs (Defra) and its Scottish and Welsh equivalents under The Wildlife and Countryside Act, 1981. You do not need to be in possession of a copy of these licences to shoot the birds concerned, but you do need to comply with the licence provisions (which include the fact that you must have permission to be on the land concerned). Also, since the licences are mostly renewed every year, you must be sure that they are still in force and that the species you wish to shoot are still listed. This is particularly relevant following devolution, and as noted below please be aware that the lists are not the same in all three countries. Naturally, the field-sports organisations such as BASC, the Countryside Alliance and the National Gamekeepers Organisation would try to keep their members up to date, but ultimately it is up to you to make sure that what you are doing remains legal. The list of species concerned is as follows:

Wood pigeon	Crow
Collared dove	Magpie
Feral pigeon	Jay
House sparrow (Scotland and Wales)	Jackdaw
Starling (Scotland and Wales)	Rook
Herring gull	Greater black-backed gull
Lesser black-backed gull	Canada Goose (England only)

Pintail – a quarry duck which may be shot during the open season.

Turning to ground game, rabbits and hares have a very strange legal status. For all practical purposes there is no closed season. However, shoot tenants over moorland and other unenclosed land may be constrained by a closed season, depending on the terms of their tenancy and who else has an interest in the land.

Sunday shooting

Shooting on a Sunday is quite widely frowned upon, but not necessarily illegal. It all depends on what you shoot and where you shoot it. Throughout England and Wales it is illegal to shoot gamebirds and hares on a Sunday, while in Scotland it is generally considered unacceptable to do so, though not strictly illegal. In Scotland, too, Sunday wildfowling is illegal, but not the shooting of rabbits or the 'pests list' of birds. South of the border, it is generally legal to shoot rabbits, the 'pests list' and wildfowl on a Sunday. There are however exceptions, and Sunday wildfowling is not allowed in the following areas of England and Wales as defined before the reorganisation of counties in 1974:

Anglesey, Brecknock, Caernarvon, Carmarthen, Cardigan, Cornwall, Denbigh, Devon, Doncaster, Glamorgan, Great Yarmouth County Borough, Isle of Ely, Leeds County Borough, Merioneth, Norfolk, Pembroke, Somerset, North and West Ridings of Yorkshire.

Many shooting leases stipulate no shooting on Sunday, even if it is otherwise legal in the area concerned. Bear in mind that shooting on Sunday is a more public event than on other days of the week, since a large proportion of the population takes a Sunday stroll after lunch. Add to this the undoubted offence which it causes to the religious, and you have an activity which is perhaps rarely in the best interests of the future of fieldsports. Dawn flight well away from housing is probably acceptable in that most people are still sleeping and therefore will not notice. Evening flight in remote areas or on a stormy night, again causes little worry. Think hard before you shoot during the day, especially if it is fine. There are six other days available each week, when even the antis expect shooting to happen.

Game licences

The Game Licences Act (1860) makes it an offence for anyone to shoot or even attempt to shoot, game without an appropriate licence. This licence, which is available from main post office branches, is needed if you wish to shoot pheasants, partridges, grouse, ptarmigan, blackgame, woodcock and snipe. In the original Act, rabbits and hares are also listed, but most persons are covered by some form of exemption. This has the effect that a game licence is only needed by poachers!

Non-toxic shot

Lead shot has been used since the invention of the shotgun. However, lead is a toxic substance. It has a particularly serious effect on waterfowl, which seem to pick it up in mistake for grit to help grind their food. It is then ground up in the gizzard, releasing lead into the bloodstream. This can kill either by direct poisoning or by debilitating the bird and making it much more vulnerable to predators.

To prevent this from happening, wildfowlers have been phasing out lead shot use over wetlands for the last fifteen years. However this voluntary approach has now been superceeded by statutory bans. In England and Wales it is illegal to use lead on a long list of wetland sites of special scientific interest, and on the foreshore. Here it is also illegal to use lead for shooting of ducks, geese, swans, coot and moorhen. Scotland has taken a rather different approach, and simply banned all use of lead in shotguns when shooting on or over wetlands. This means that lead can still be used, for example when shooting geese over dry stubbles, but that lead would be illegal for a pheasant flushed from a flooded marsh.

Selling game

Most rough shooters will only be shooting for the pot, or to give a brace away to friends. If you wish to sell your game you either need a game dealer's licence yourself, or you must only sell to a licensed game dealer. This provision applies to gamebirds, rabbits, hares, deer, woodcock and snipe, but not to duck, golden plover or pigeons. Also, it is illegal to sell dead wild geese.

Insurance protection

There is no legal obligation upon anyone to have public liability insurance when shooting. However, when one considers the potential damage which a shotgun can do, anyone who shoots without insurance protection is taking a very severe risk if an accident does happen. Public liability insurance is easy to arrange, and is an automatic benefit offering cover to £5 million for all BASC and Countryside Alliance members. Aside from the good work which these organisations do for the shooting community, the peace of mind offered by this insurance alone is worth the annual subscriptions. This should in no way tempt you ever to take a chancy shot. Scrupulous attention to safety is *essential* at all times.

Respect for the quarry

Whenever you take up your gun, consider the truth of the view that game is there to be cropped, rather than to be exploited. Taking a reasonable harvest is fair, but attempting to get every last one that you can is likely to impose excessive strain on the population and lead to a long-term decline. Do not be greedy, especially about migrants like woodcock and wildfowl. Remember that many other sportsmen will probably have taken their share of the population too during the long autumn migration.

Most sportsmen would consider it quite wrong to shoot a bird on the ground. Certainly, in the case of gamebirds like pheasants, partridge and woodcock, a large part of the sport is in the test of marksmanship which a fast-flying bird offers. In the case of wildfowl, the decision might be slightly different. After a long and careful crawl for a wild duck which you have seen drop, you might consider it reasonable to take a shot at a bird still sitting on the water. Similarly, a pigeon which you have carefully stalked in its roosting tree. The decision is really a personal one, and there is certainly no legal guidance on the matter. Whatever you do, however, do not be tempted by a long shot. If it is not inside the range where accurate shooting means a clean kill, it certainly is not sporting to take a shot. The only time when such a long shot is in any way justified is when you attempt to dispatch an already wounded animal before it escapes. In this respect if you are alone, a *safe* shot at a hobbling rabbit, running pheasant or diving duck is perfectly sensible. Such things are only frowned upon at formal shoots because there are so many people and dogs around, and the safety risks are too high.

The other person's sport

If you shoot alone, any fair offer is yours, but when you are in company think of the other Guns too. Would that pheasant make a better shot for someone else? Have you had more than your share of sport already? Do not just say to yourself it is safe, it is in range, it is legal, bang. A pheasant lumbering into the air in front of you is a fairly easy shot, but it might offer far more sport for your neighbour once it has gained both height and speed.

There are other considerations too. For example, at dawn flight around a lake, the mallard are circling high, but just in range. Do not just take the first offer: think, will they drop lower? In so doing they may well offer your companion a better chance, and then perhaps come back over you on their way out. On another occasion you are sharing a wood for roosting pigeons. The same rule applies, he who pulls on birds at extreme range spoils the game for everyone. Do not be greedy or you will rapidly become unpopular, and you will not get asked back.

Which brings me to 'Thank you' letters. Why do so few people bother these days? If you have had a good day as someone's guest, put pen to paper and say so. It brings back happy memories for your host too.

The public perception

More people use the countryside each and every year. Most of them seem to have a decreasing regard for rights of property, and so they choose to ignore whether there is a public right of way or not. There is a fair chance that they are anti-shooting as well. You therefore have the option of either hardening or softening their attitude.

To start with, be scrupulously safe with your gun. Do not shoot low through the woods. Do not shoot pigeons right at the end of someone's garden, allowing the bang of your gun and the fall out of shot to upset them all afternoon. Also, whenever you meet a member of the public in your ramblings, break and unload your gun, just as you would in a shooting party. If people are where they should not be, perhaps with the dog ranging widely off the lead, point it out politely. Be firm, by all means, but start with 'Good Morning . . .' not 'Oi, what the hell . . .'. If you explain the problems, the damage and the risks to them in a helpful way, you stand a chance of mending their ways. If you lay down the law you may have got rid of them for now, but you will have hardened their attitude against the sport. Remember to be particularly careful what you say about the dog. There is only one way I know of to offend someone even more than by accusing them of being a bad driver, and that is telling them that they have got a bad dog. 'Billy' may have slight faults, but he is the most intelligent dog in the world *and* a paragon of virtue really. The same applies with gundogs too, but that is another story.

The Code of Good Shooting Practice

All of these ethical considerations, plus much more besides, are the subject of a joint code of practice. The Code of Good Shooting Practice was first published in the early 1990s and the most recent edition came out in 2003. It is supported by all the fieldsports organisations and many others, and is freely available. Everyone who shoots should obtain a copy, read it, and follow its spirit at all times. By doing so, we go a long way to keeping our own house in order, and avoiding restrictive legislation promoted by those who oppose us.

Section 2
QUARRY AND THEIR PURSUIT

7

Pheasants

'There can be no doubt whatever that whether as a maid in her first season or as a juvenile matron, the hen is infinitely superior to the cock.'

A. Innes Shand 'The Cookery of the Pheasant'. In *The Pheasant*, Fur and Feather Series (1895)

Origins

The pheasant is by far our most common gamebird, and The Game Conservancy Trust estimates that pheasants form at least 70 per cent of all the quarry shot in the United Kingdom. This figure will seem incredible to the rough shooter of West Wales, who may never see a single pheasant from beginning to end of a season in his wanderings after woodcock and bunnies. What makes the figure even more surprising is the fact that the pheasant is an introduced species of Asian origin.

Exactly when the first pheasants were brought to the British Isles is lost in the mists of time. It is certainly true that the Romans were familiar with the pheasant, but whether they ever brought them across the Channel is not clear. In any case their interest was purely in raising them for the table. The Romans certainly did not engage in anything so crazy as letting pheasants go and then chasing them for sport!

It is far more likely that the first pheasants to reach these shores came with the Normans, the Romans having only established them in Italy, Germany and France. Whenever they arrived, they were certainly breeding in the wild by the fifteenth century. Even so, they were probably not widespread until the late eighteenth century, and only really became an important game species in the nineteenth.

The native range of the pheasant extends from the eastern shore of the Caspian sea, to eastern China, with a separate closely related species, the Japanese green pheasant in Japan. Over the years various authorities have

described an enormous selection of subspecies mainly based on plumage varieties in cock birds.

It is clear that the original introductions were of the nominate race, *Phasianus colchicus colchicus*, which is the westernmost form, coming from the Caspian area. This is the familiar black necked or Old English variety. Since then a series of other introductions of different forms have occurred, including the Chinese ring necked (*P c torquatus*), the very pale, mongolian (*P c mongolicus*) and the Prince of Wales pheasant (*P c principalis*) which is similar to the mongolian, but with a less pronounced white neck ring.

The result is that our pheasants have a distinctly muddled pedigree, and might reasonably be described as a bunch of mongrels. Also, captive breeding has been a major part of their history, and in common with most captive bred livestock, various 'sports' or mutants have turned up. Perhaps the most familiar is the very striking, near black 'melanistic' form – a colour type which extends to the hens as well, producing deep chocolate colours with coppery tones in place of the usual sandy browns. At the other end of the scale there are very pale 'leucistic' forms, often called bohemians, and pure whites which may

The black-necked or Old English Pheasant. The first race to have been introduced to Britain. *(Terence Blank)*

or may not qualify as albinos. The distinction here is that a true albino has no pigmentation whatever, and thus shows a pink eye. Most white pheasants have a normal brown eye and red wattles.

More recently there have been a confusing array of new introductions. These have been aimed at improving the flying quality following what many perceive as a decline over the last 30 or so years. The common consensus, backed up by some science, is that generations of breeding from 'caught-up' birds, which the guns refused to shoot, has produced large, lazy pheasants.

In response there has been a series of fads, starting with wild fen pheasants from East Anglia and followed by Scandinavians (supposed wild birds from certain islands in the Baltic). Then came Japanese green crosses, followed by Michigan blue-backs (Chinese ring-necked pheasants, probably mainly from France, but looking the same as those introduced to Michigan to improve the local wild strain). All this need hardly bother the rough shooter, for in the long run it just adds to the variability of our mongrels. However, two points are worth making. First, the only 'real' type here is the Japanese green, which has been described as a distinct species. Otherwise, pheasants are no more native in Michigan or Scandinavia than in the U.K., so the rest of these types still originate from Asia. Secondly, if you rear birds for the shoot and want good performance, decide on a quality breeding programme and do not use caught-up leftovers. There would have been no need for any of these recent introductions if we had got the breeding policy right in the first place.

Natural history

In biological terms the pheasant is not so very different from its near relative the chicken. It is a ground nesting bird which, when adult, feeds on a mainly vegetable diet of seeds and shoots. In common with the chicken it has the habit of spending its nights roosting off the ground if nature provides a suitable roost, thus reducing its chances of being caught asleep by a fox or similar ground predator. Unlike the more domestic chicken, the pheasant is a strong and fast flier if the need arises. However, given the choice, it would almost always walk or run rather than fly perhaps because it has only limited endurance in the air. Just like the human sprinter, the pheasant is capable of only a very short burst of power flight before it is forced to set its wings and plane on to land. On an average, this power flight will last for about 8 seconds only, but that is quite long enough for the bird to cover about 200 yards, during which it can reach a height of at least 150 feet, if necessary. From such a level, it can plane on for probably a quarter of a mile over flat country, and much further if the contours allow. Having completed such a 'marathon' its powers of flight are nearly exhausted, and it needs an hour or so to recover before another similar flight can be attempted.

As far as habitat preferences are concerned, the pheasant in its native land is a bird of the scrub, reed-beds and swamps. In the United Kingdom the same basic preferences apply, with scrub and woodland edges forming the favoured

Pheasants usually nest on the ground. *(Terence Blank)*

habitat. Pheasants rarely stray far into the centre of large woods even in winter and positively avoid such places in summer unless there are really large clearings or wide rides. A forest track with little or no gap in the canopy is not adequate.

Fortunately for the shooting man, pheasants are not the brightest of birds. In fact, their intelligence is fairly low compared to ducks, geese or even pigeons. Hence the fact that they can be driven out of a wood over a line of Guns, and still return to the same wood an hour later. Even so they are comparatively wary birds, especially if of wild rather than hand-reared origin. You only need to peer round the corner of a hedge and watch birds up to 200 yards away run for cover to realise that their wariness is combined with good eyesight.

A noisy approach sends them scuttling for cover too. In fact, they have remarkably good hearing especially of lower frequencies. A graphic illustration of this was given by Brian Vesey Fitzgerald in *British Game* (1946). He noted pheasants crowing in Hampshire when London was being bombed during the Second World War, even though he could not hear the bombing himself. Similarly, in Japan, pheasant crowing is taken as an indication of an impending earthquake. Hence the value to the rough shooter of a dog which works to hand signals and quiet whistles. Shouting your orders only announces your approach in time for the pheasants to slink off down the hedge and away.

Hen pheasants produce a large clutch of rather uniform pale-olive coloured eggs. These can have a tinge of green, brown or even blue. The chicks which hatch from these eggs are mobile within a few hours of emergence, and follow their mother in pursuit of food. In common with all the other gamebirds about which we know, the chicks feed principally on insects for the first few weeks of life. This diet provides the protein which is essential for the rapid growth which these birds need. The chicks themselves are capable of flying, if rather weakly, from only 10 or 12 days old, but continue to grow until aged about 14 to 16 weeks. At this stage the cock poults will be larger than their mother, and the hens almost as large. Indeed the latter may well be very difficult to distinguish, but cocks will still have a rather scruffy plumage for another week or two.

Walked-up pheasants

Most of the time the rough shooter in pursuit of pheasants will be hunting alone, or with a chosen companion. In such situations there will be no helpers apart from a dog or two. All sport will be as a direct result of the sportsman's own efforts. For best results a carefully planned strategy is needed.

As mentioned earlier, the pheasant is no intellectual, but it is a wary bird. Too much noise in the approach is definitely not a help. A quiet Gun with a businesslike dog which does not need too much direction is far more likely to catch a bird by surprise. At 200 yards, a pheasant which hears or sees your approach will run, and if you follow will keep on running for a long way. However, given some cover, the bird which suddenly rumbles you when you are only some 30 yards away will probably squat and hide, relying on its camouflage and stillness to elude you. However, this lack of movement does not completely cover the scent. If your dog is any good, it will probably catch a touch of scent, hunt the bird, and flush it for you well within range.

So, keep your voice down. Use whatever cover is available to screen your approach. Watch where you put your feet to avoid cracking dry sticks, and use the wind. An upwind approach blows the noise of your movements away from your quarry. It also gives your dog much more chance to pick up a touch of scent wafting down on the wind, and a touch of scent is all that a good dog needs to get it homing in on your bird.

Hedges and ditches

When you finally flush a bird, the odds are that it will slip out on the wrong side of whatever cover is available and elude your shot. When you are alone, this is especially difficult to overcome. The pheasant hears your approach and automatically decides that the quiet side is a better bet. Also, the bird has probably been lurking in the thickest piece of cover for miles around, so the obstruction is bigger than elsewhere along the hedge too. If there are two of you the problem does not arise. One gun on each side of the hedge, the dog in the cover, and so long as it does not hunt too far ahead everything should flush in range and give at least one of you a chance.

Learn to work *with* your dog, more pheasants will find their way into your bag. *(John Marchington)*

What happens if you are alone, how do you decide which side to walk? There can be no guarantees but some general principles do apply. Firstly, birds take off into the wind. You will, of course, try to hunt into the wind, but even so, it will rarely blow straight along your hedge or ditch, so put yourself on the upwind side. Most dogs will tend to want to hunt on the lee side anyway. Their own instinct and experience tells them that this is the best place to catch maximum game scent for minimum effort. The dog which crashes into the far side of the hedge is likely to push game to your side anyway, and if it then takes off into the wind, a fair offer should be yours.

A second principle which can help is that pheasants tend to want to head for 'home' when flushed. Home is usually the wood or other covert in which they choose to roost. If they are of hand-reared origin, it is also likely to be the one from which they were released.

A further consideration comes into play when walking up a hedge and ditch combined, or even a hedge with a more extensive rough bank on one side than the other. In such cases, a greater proportion of the birds will probably be on the side with the most cover, so this is the best side to choose, other things being equal.

And lastly, there is experience. In the end this is probably the best guide. If the birds usually go a particular way when you hunt a certain piece of cover, place yourself accordingly. At worst you will force some wily old cock to change his plans, and you might just improve your chances of a shot.

If all these factors add up to a dilemma, and they usually do, I would choose whatever previous experience tells me first. However, the wind factor comes a very close second, particularly if your dog is one of those who has the happy habit of understanding the idea of working the other side of the hedge and pushing things to you. Some never achieve it, others seem to find it of their own accord, and some can be trained to work in this way. I suspect many more could be so trained if only more people would recognise the value of such skills.

Big woods

I have already mentioned that the pheasant is a bird of the woodland edge. This is illustrated well in a wood of 280 acres which some friends and I shoot over in southern Wiltshire. It is mainly broadleafed plantation, with a few small compartments of up to an acre or so of conifers, plus a large area of mixed larch, fir, beech and ash. The wood is surrounded by a mix of arable, downland, and two areas of woodland which march directly with it.

No pheasants are released into our wood, nor indeed on any of the adjacent farms, so an average morning with the dog results in flushing no more than one or two pheasants, and often these do not present a safe shot. Over the last five seasons a consistent pattern has emerged. At least 90 per cent of the birds seen are located within 20 yards of the boundary. None are found along those parts which march with neighbouring woods. The remaining 10 per cent come from the several clearings, or on the edges between conifer and broadleaf blocks. Hunting around under the mature beech forest is a total waste of time, and even the one patch of oak with hazel scrub in the middle is a poor prospect. Just occasionally one finds a bird along the southern edge of this patch alongside a fairly wide ride.

In midwinter, especially if the weather is wild and really cold, it is worth poking around the small conifer blocks early in the morning. The pheasants seem to use these as roosts in such conditions, and they may hang around for a while before going off to spend the day in the fields and hedges. Under normal circumstances, however, even these areas are a dead loss. Unless the weather is really inclement, the pheasants roost in trees near the outside edge, and they are off down the hedges by breakfast time, not returning until late afternoon.

Now personally, I am of the opinion that one of the best ways to drive a pheasant away is to disturb it at roost. I therefore do most of my shooting in this particular wood at around sunrise. An hour working the better edges at this time can make a most enjoyable start to a winter day, perhaps before going off to spend the day picking-up on a more formal affair, or even to 'drive a desk' in the office. If I do not have any pressing engagements to go on to, I work the clearings in case a bird has elected to stay there. Also, several of these areas are chosen by woodcock as a daytime resting place, and I will forget all thoughts of pheasants if I think there is a chance of the former offering a shot.

Sadly, cold wet weather gives a much better chance in this wood. If it is a miserable day, the pheasants will be far more likely to choose the shelter of the wood and scratch round there for grub. Somehow, however, such weather just does not seem to accord with our ideas of ideal game shooting conditions. There is no doubt that wet pheasants do not fly so well anyway, and driven shooting in really wet weather is a miserable business. Sadly, it seems to be so rare to hear of anyone cancelling a day in such conditions these days.

For the rough shooter, however, such problems are not quite so serious, a slight reluctance to fly may mean that birds flush in range rather than beyond

Small parties can often increase their success by sending one or two folk to stand forward. *(John Marchington)*

it. However, I really cannot get frightfully enthusiastic about hunting pheasants in the dripping woods. I may be reducing my chances, but I much prefer a crisp frosty day.

Small drives

As soon as there are two or more Guns, it pays to consider whether the best strategy is to split up and work in such a way that you are likely to drive a bird over your companion and *vice versa*. This may not always be the best policy, but it is a trick which you are well advised to have up your sleeve when needed. The plan starts with the boundary hedge. If you do not have permission to shoot on the neighbour's side, why not start from opposite ends? At least this will mean that the game in the hedge is caught in a 'pincer' manoeuvre. They will all have to flush, and none can run on ahead for ever. Those which escape on the wrong side would be lost anyway, but at least you stand to gain a shot at some of those which might never have flown.

Other circumstances may present too. In the wood mentioned earlier, there is a dilapidated rabbit fence around most of the boundary. Pheasants on the inside of this will often run ahead and either find a way through or flush out of shot. Standing one Gun at a corner of the fence while the other walks a 200 yard section towards him can pay off. This is especially so if the standing Gun takes a position in the bottom of the one valley which runs through the shoot. Some very satisfying high-driven birds have been shot (and missed!) in this way.

As the size of the party increases, splitting up becomes more and more likely to improve sport. One group can go on ahead, and push the far hedge into a covert, while the others walk-up the two near hedges and then drive the birds over the advance party. In carrying out such a manoeuvre, it is important that the advance party give the main covert a wide berth in skirting round to their forward positions. At least 100 yards out are needed if they are not to risk alerting some of the birds and send them running down the very hedge which they are about to head off. You might get away with a closer approach at the start of the season, but such liberties in January will not work. Advance planning is also essential to such manoeuvres, since both parties must know exactly what they are doing. Any question of shouted orders across two ploughed fields is a recipe for disaster. Someone will end up in the wrong place, and anyway it will all be academic, since the birds will have been scared into the next parish by the din.

Such party affairs will also call for greater attention to etiquette and safety. You have not just got your own sport to think about, but also everyone else's too. Do not be greedy, and do not shoot birds going forward if you are part of the walking party. Those in wait out front may have a long wait for their shot, and the bird is almost bound to be more exciting for them than you, provided that you have not cut it down as it lurches into the air at your feet.

The rough shooter who is used to walked-up birds will need to school himself if such drives are to go well. When hunting alone, you are not all that concerned about where the birds will want to go. However, if your standing Guns are to have some fun, at least some of the birds must go forward, so the rules about 'home woods' already mentioned must be observed. If there are no such areas, perhaps because all the birds are wild, at least be sure to try to drive your birds towards some suitable covert. If you try to push them out into entirely open country, they are very unlikely to go. There must be cover of some sort, even if it is only a reed-fringed ditch, a scrub-filled pit-hole, or a gappy hedge.

The order in which you work your ground is important too. As noted earlier, most pheasants will roost off the ground if they get the chance. Thus, they tend to spend the night in the woods. However, they will often spread out into the local countryside quite early in the morning. In so doing they make use of rough banks, hedges, small patches of scrub, river and stream banks, and any standing crops, including those deliberately planted for them. However, having had a good feed in these areas, they will usually begin to draw back towards their roosting coverts by mid-afternoon, having a last feed here before bedtime. You should therefore plan your assault so that any such outlying coverts are

A few non-shooting volunteers can be a great help, but do ensure that they will see the sport. (*John Marchington*)

shot during the morning, or at the latest soon after lunch. Woodland drives can then follow to end the day – always bearing in mind the vital importance of finishing early so that your pheasants have plenty of time to go to roost.

Also, do not forget what was mentioned earlier about the pheasant being a 'sprinter'; it needs a reasonable recovery time between flights to give of its best. Doing a return drive straight away is a mistake. Any birds which have flown in from the previous covert will be very likely to either flop out low, go back low between the beaters, or worse still get themselves caught by your dogs. It is much better to go off and do another drive elsewhere and risk a few birds walking out if you have no one available to stop off the covert in question until later in the day.

Stops and beaters

Rough shoots will rarely be so grand as to have the resources to employ beaters as such. Indeed they really cease to qualify as rough shoots if they do. However, it is not unusual for a rough shooting syndicate of seven or eight Guns to be able to muster a few keen helpers. These volunteers, be they young shots who are not yet allowed to shoot in company, or just friends who like a day in the fresh air, are an invaluable help.

Naturally enough, they will mostly want to be where the action is – in the line of walking Guns. However, given a careful briefing, most will be prepared to spend a little time on stop somewhere; for example, standing and quietly tapping a stick on the main hedge which exits a covert reserved for later. In this way, they can make a much more valuable contribution to the success of the day than by being in the beating line.

Discretion will be needed to get the best out of such people, and you must expect protests if you ask the same unfortunate soul to spend the whole day, getting cold and miserable in a series of long boring waits. So, always remember to rotate such jobs between the team – and thank them properly afterwards. If they feel that they are a key part of the team, and understand what they are doing, they will find the whole thing much more enjoyable. This is especially so if they are positioned so that they can see some shooting going on as well. Teamwork and organisation of this type can make the whole day much more successful. It also makes for greater enjoyment for all concerned, not least because you do not suffer the inevitable stress when things go wrong.

Cocks only

The pheasant is rather different from the rest of the species in this book in one important aspect of breeding biology – one cock bird is quite capable of mating with many hens. Full fertility in the wild has been recorded when the sex ratio falls as low as 1 cock to 12 hens, while ratios as low as 1 in 50 have worked in captivity. For this reason it is perfectly possible to shoot a high proportion of cocks without interfering with the population or its productivity. Indeed, there are many keepers who would assert that an excess of cocks is bad for wild breeding due to squabbling cocks disturbing the hens. This has led to tradition of 'cocks only' days at the end of the season, designed to reduce their population. There is no real scientific evidence as to whether this is really important to wild breeding success. However, it is certainly true that shooting more cocks than hens is a sensible way of obtaining the maximum yield from a pheasant population whether wild or hand reared. One aspect of this which is worthy of consideration is to shoot cocks only early in the season when the population is at its highest. This has the dual advantage of allowing an assessment of how many hens there are on the ground, and leaving them for later so as to spread the sport more evenly over the season.

8

Partridges

'The two most important distinguishing features of the partridge which set it apart from other birds are not the plumage, but the excitement it gives as a quarry species and its delectable flavour.'

G. R. Potts *The Partridge: Pesticides, predation and conservation* (1986)

Origins

In the United Kingdom today, we have two species of partridge, the introduced redleg or French and our native Grey. The latter is often given the misnomer English, which must be pretty offensive if you are Scottish, Welsh or Irish, since the grey partridge is just as much a native, if sadly declined in status, in all those parts.

In common with the pheasant, the grey partridge has been introduced around the world to various countries. Most of these imports have been of Hungarian rather than British stock, the grey having a native distribution over much of Europe and western Asia. Thus half the world call our greys Hungarian partridges, or worse still 'Huns' for short. Since the redleg also comes from Spain, Portugal and some other southern European countries, I shall stick to redlegs for the one, and greys for the others in this book. At least in that way no one's national pride will be dented!

Natural history

Lumping these two species together in one account is a dangerous thing to do. There are inevitably many similarities between what are, after all, two quite closely-related birds. However, there are differences too, some of which are very important to the rough shooter. The grey is very much a bird of open country, its natural habitat clearly being open grasslands of the sort typified by steppe country. No doubt its native United Kingdom habitat was sand dunes, chalk downland and the edges of the moors. However, with the advent of arable farming a new habitat was opening up, and the grey partridge is now typically a bird of the cornlands, although many other habitats are frequented.

The redleg, however, is less tied to open country. While it does well enough in open areas, particularly if they have good hedges, it will also take to scrubby country quite readily. Indeed, in its native areas in southern Europe, the redleg is very much an inhabitant of scrub, maquis, orchards and olive groves. It is also much more inclined to perch off the ground. If you see a partridge running along a wall, standing on a rick, or strutting about on the roof of a barn, it will be a redleg. Clearly, it was the redleg rather than the grey which took to the pear tree for the Christmas song.

Since its introduction to East Anglia in the 1770s the redleg has spread over a wide area of England, and it is generally considered to be fully naturalised and self-sustaining south and east of a line from Yorkshire to Dorset. There are also pockets of country north and west of this line, and particularly in Eastern Scotland, where the redleg may well be self-sustaining too. However, since it is regularly released in considerable numbers over a much wider area than this it is impossible to say exactly where the limits of naturalisation are.

In more recent times hybrids between the redleg and its near relative the chukar have been widely released in this country. However, it has become clear that, although these birds are easy to breed in the game-farm situation, their

The grey partridge is a native of the whole of the British and Irish mainland. *(Terence Blank)*

Since its introduction over two centuries ago, the redleg has colonised much of the south and east. *(Terence Blank)*

productivity in the wild is so low that they would become extinct without annual releasing. They can also interbreed with the pure redleg, which could have an adverse effect on this species too. For this reason it became illegal to release both the chukar and its hybrids in 1992.

In common with the pheasant, both species of partridge are ground nesting, although the occasional redleg will choose a slightly elevated position such as a stack of bales or the top of a pile of rubbish. Grey partridges have the distinction of producing the highest average clutch size of any bird – about 15 eggs. The redleg usually produces a somewhat smaller clutch of about a dozen. However, some redleg hens will lay two separate clutches one of which they incubate whilst the other is incubated by the cock. The two birds sometimes get together with their joint brood after hatching. Needless to say the cock grey has nothing to do with such continental practices, but he does help with the brooding and rearing once his family hatch out.

Insects are a vital food for newly hatched partridges. *(Terence Blank)*

In common with all the other gamebirds about which we know, newly-hatched partridge chicks feed mainly on insects. The redleg appears to be less dependent on them but grey partridge chicks need at least 95 per cent insects in their diet for their early days if they are to thrive.

Sadly, in today's intensive farm environment, insect populations are usually far lower than they used to be, and as a result the large partridge coveys of former days are something of a rarity. Indeed, chick survival is so low in most areas that the partridge population is barely 'ticking over'. Here they are often at such a low level that shooting is largely a waste of time, and also potentially a threat to the tiny remaining stock.

Fortunately, in the last 15 years or so, The Game Conservancy Trust has come up with an answer: the conservation headland. This is a strip around the edge of a cereal field which is cropped as normal, but on which most of the sprays are not used. The result is the perfect partridge brood-rearing habitat – a mix of growing cereals and a few weeds, which is full of just the right insects for chick food. It also helps the conservation of an enormous range of other wildlife from small mammals to butterflies, and it often contains rare wildflowers too. As this technique is more and more widely adopted, it seems certain that we shall see an improvement in the fortunes of our native partridges as well as the redlegs and indeed also wild pheasants.

Good brood-rearing habitat can also be created on set-aside land. By sowing a mix of cereals and broad-leaved crops such as linseed or rape, an artificial conservation headland can be created under what is known as the 'wild bird cover option'.

Habits

As mentioned earlier, partridges are largely ground-living birds and, in common with pheasants, they normally prefer to walk and run rather than fly. However, they do habitually fly a little more often than pheasants. Greys, for example, usually fly out 100 yards or so to their night-time 'roost' site. This, no doubt, helps to foil ground predators which might otherwise steal up to a sleeping covey by following their scent trail.

When pursued by Guns and dogs, both species of partridge will normally run on ahead if they spot approaching danger soon enough. However, redlegs seem prone to running further and faster, a characteristic which made them very unpopular in the last century with sportsmen who shot partridges over pointers. Redlegs also have a strong tendency to run into cover before flushing. Thus, when a team of Guns enter a field containing a covey of this species, the birds will often run on into the far hedge, and flush out of the far side. Greys, however, tend to squat in the field itself, and then flush. The first flush is often outside gunshot range, but if you meet the covey again, it may well sit for longer. Also, wild-bred greys in particular, can only be pushed so far. Eventually they will feel that they have gone far enough from home, and they will either fly round the end of the line, or back over it. All of these habits have major implications for both walking-up and driving.

Walking-up

Walked-up partridge shooting is a dying art. Few landowners have sufficient wild stocks to do it in all but exceptional years, and most people who release birds do so primarily for driving. However, there are still a few places where the time-honoured practice of walking the September stubbles with pointers or setters is carried out. As mentioned earlier, redlegs can be most frustrating when treated in this way, but hunting coveys of wild greys in weedy stubbles is enormously satisfying. Provided that the coveys are sitting well, small parties and even lone Guns can have superb sport over pointing dogs. Otherwise, and especially when no pointing dogs are available, walking-up partridges is really a job for a party, since most of the birds will be able to run rings round the lone sportsman.

Occasionally, early in the season, greys in particular will sit tight enough to allow the lone Gun the odd shot, but as time goes on they will get progessively wilder, and more inclined to run. In these circumstances, a party walking in line will be far more effective. Even if coveys flush out of shot to start with, they are more inclined either to sit tight for longer, or to try to break back when the party comes upon them again.

People who know their ground and birds well, have a good idea of where the quarry will want to go when first flushed, and will take their beat in that direction. For the first half an hour there may be very little shooting with most coveys flushing out of range, but as time progresses more and more of the coveys will have flown once or twice, so the pace of sport will quicken.

An extension of this technique is to walk several areas of open ground towards a patch of cover, and then work the cover very carefully. A classic example of this is sugar beet. Grey partridges do not normally like this crop very much. But when disturbed, they will often choose a beet field as escape

Redlegs are quite easy to release, but provide rather poor sport when walked up.

cover when flushed, and hold much tighter in this than on more open stubbles or winter corn. The trick, then, is to walk the neighbouring fields into the beet and then to hunt the beet itself. The question of how much help you need from dogs in this kind of sport is a little vexed. If you have no cover to which to drive your birds, you are probably best off with all dogs walking to heel. So long as the Guns are no more than a gunshot apart, it will be rare for a covey to sit so tight that your team walks past them, and even close-working dogs may well flush out of reach. Also, if a covey jumps and goes off low, a dog invariably gets in the way, which means no one gets a shot. However, when you are hunting thicker cover, such as sugar beet, birds can sit incredibly tight. In these circumstances good close-working dogs are essential if you are to get the maximum amount of sport.

Whatever happens the party should have retrieving dogs with them anyway, and all shot birds should be searched for the moment they fall. In the warm conditions which often prevail with early autumn shooting, scenting can be notoriously bad, so give your dogs the maximum chance by getting them on to the fall of a bird as soon as possible. The one exception is the bird which flies on apparently unscathed to tower or drop out a couple of hundred yards ahead in the beat which you are taking. In this case, sending dogs straight away may well spoil other chances by flushing birds out of shot. Such birds invariably fall dead anyway, so they should be retrievable as long as the fall is accurately marked. A good plan is for two or more widely-spaced members of the line to mark the direction of the fall, and their position at the time. If the bird is not easily found, you can return later, and walk from these marked positions in the pre-set direction. Where the lines cross is then a good mark for the fall. The problem with this is remembering where you were exactly at the time of the fall. Flattening a few square yards of the crop will not be popular, so why not carry a few pieces of rag in your pocket to drop in such circumstances? This works well only on calm days. Another alternative, if there is a non-shooting member of the party, is to ask them to carry a few cane markers with a piece of coloured rag attached.

Mention was made earlier of spacing Guns at no more than 40 yards to avoid any risk of birds being missed. Slightly wider spacing might be alright at the start of a beat, when birds are not expected to flush within shot. This allows a wider piece of country to be covered. However, once the shooting starts in earnest it is a mistake to try and take in too large a piece of ground. If Guns are 50 or 60 yards apart when the birds flush, there is a strong risk that they will be unable to get a safe shot. Any coveys heading back will be likely to come through low, half-way between the Guns. They will only really be in range when passing through the line, when safety considerations preclude a shot. The result is wasted chances, or a strong temptation to take limit of range shots at departing birds. There is thus a very high risk of wounding, which is unacceptable.

This kind of walking in line is far less satisfactory with redlegs for the reasons already mentioned. In most cases, if the size of the party allows, it is best to split into two teams and try to engineer small drives. An exception, where there are only two or three guns is to take advantage of the redleg's propensity to run for cover. If you run a covey or two into a hedge or dyke, it can be worthwhile to then walk the hedge up with a Gun on each side and a close working dog or two in the cover. With luck, the birds will eventually flush and give one or other side a shot. This works especially well in gappy hedges, or those which are blind-ended, or simply run in to a fence line. In all such cases the partridges eventually find that the cover runs out, and are forced to take wing. Similar strategies involving other cover, such as pit-holes, rough banks, and patches of scrub will suggest themselves to those who have such features on their ground. Such sport can be rather disappointing, since redlegs flushed in this way will rarely fly well. In most cases driving is a better strategy.

Small drives

Full-blown partridge driving is obviously outside the scope of this book. However, rough shooters with partridges on their ground can often provide themselves with a taste of driven birds even when the party of Guns is very small. Successful drives can even be had by just two Guns, provided that they know where a covey lives, and where it will want to go when flushed. In these circumstances, one Gun chooses a stand under the line of flight and his companion walks the covey up and pushes it over him.

Whatever the size of the party, this local knowledge is the key to success. Most partridge coveys have a distinct home range, whether redleg or grey. Once flushed, they will usually have a favoured route of escape. This may vary according to wind direction, and it is a general rule that it is easiest to push partridges downwind. However, provided that the wind is not too strong, it is often possible to drive birds *straight* into it. Given a crosswind, birds will tend to side-slip, and this should be taken into account when planning drives (of which more later).

Even hand-reared partridges can hear, and they will be much less likely to go forward if the Guns make a noise when getting into position. Stealth in the field seems to be a sadly forgotten art these days, which is a pity. Creeping stealthily into position improves the chances of success in the drive, *and* it adds to the excitement and anticipation. It also means that the walking team can be less noisy in their approach, since they will not have to work so hard at driving the birds over the forward Guns.

Provided that the standing team have got into position quietly, the walkers will be able to be quite widely spaced at the start of a drive. Their appearance at the skyline should send coveys running towards the main flushing area of the drive, and the 'net' will have been closed before they decide to flush. In this situation, even if they decide to go back, someone will get a shot. One of the keys to success, however, is to ensure that the flanks of the walking team join up with those standing as soon as possible. Then, if there has been a little too

Non-shooting helpers on partridge days should be issued with a flag.

much noise up front, and birds try to leak out of the sides, there will be no gap.

If you are lucky enough to have a few non-shooting helpers, they can play a far more active role than that explained with pheasants. In partridge driving you are far better off to include them in the walking team, and to issue them with flags.

A simple design is to use half of a white plastic fertiliser (or fish food) bag attached to a hazel rod. A more sophisticated version, in fluorescent orange is available from The Game Conservancy Trust. In either case, those with a flag should be told to keep it furled at their side, in readiness for a sudden and vigorous wave if any of the birds try to head out of the beat. Waiting until the birds are on the wing, and only 50 yards away, gives real surprise value and turns coveys well. Showing the flag too early leads to familiarity, and we all know that familiarity breeds contempt.

The first place to have No. 1 flag (if you only have one person) is on the downwind flank, in an attempt to push the birds out over the standing team. Then No. 2 flag is on the opposite flank, and others can be distributed evenly between the walking Guns. In a really strong crosswind, it pays to consider two flags together on the downwind flank, and to allow them to 'cut-off' some of the Guns. The birds will swing and fly down the line anyway, so those who have been cut off will still be in the shooting.

Another important point of strategy with partridges is in return drives. Unlike the pheasant, partridges can be flown again almost immediately. Indeed if you have pushed some coveys away from home, and wish to return them for another drive you should do so straight away. If you do not, they probably go back on foot, and you will hear them laughing behind you when you come to this drive later in the day. Thus the basic rule for partridges is very different from pheasants. For these smaller birds you should plan your day on the basis of drive, return, drive, return, with no gaps to go and do other places while the birds rest.

Redlegs are a little different from greys. They are slower fliers, coveys are more inclined to split up, and they often run further. If you only have one species you will be able to modify your plans accordingly, but if you have both, you will have to compromise.

One of the worst compromises is over driving hedges. A tall hedge is the perfect place to show greys, with the standing Guns 30 yards out, and really fast snap shooting as the coveys come fizzing over the hedge. Unfortunately, redlegs will often run into the hedge and only flush from the base, coming low between the Guns and offering third-rate sport. One possible solution is to get permission to grow a little mustard as a post-harvest 'catch crop' a little way back from the hedge. Given cover such as this redlegs are much more likely to flush before they reach the hedge, and come over in the same way as greys. Otherwise, your best bet is probably to try and use any sudden changes of contour on your ground. Redlegs will often flush and fly over a sudden drop rather than walk or run any further, especially if there is a little cover in the form of rough ground or hedge along the top of the ridge. In all cases, beware standing your Guns too far back. Both species of partridge have a tendency to follow the contours rather than cross them, so Guns should not be out of shot of the feature. If they are, the birds may well fly along in front of them, tantalisingly close but just out of range. In such circumstances the temptation to shoot is great, and this can lead both to pricked birds and shots low over the heads of the walking team. Whenever the walking team breasts such a ridge they should hold any flags up high or otherwise signal their approach to the forward Guns so as to ensure that there is no risk of tragedy.

Shootable stocks

In an area where there are good partridge stocks, there can be a strong temptation to go on shooting beyond what the population can sustain. With hand-reared birds it is normal to expect a return of about 40 per cent from the birds released. This should still leave a nucleus population for wild breeding for the subsequent season, provided that the birds have been well looked after at release time. *However, wild populations can rarely sustain such a heavy toll.* Those landowners with a population of wild partridges should take the trouble to carry out a spring pair count in March, and follow this up by counting coveys in August, after harvest. This second count, which is carried out from a vehicle, aims to sample the population and tell the proportion of young and old birds. Remember to count all birds, including 'barren pairs' and single old cocks. Also, check that coveys really do consist of two parents and however many young. Failed breeders often tack on to other coveys, and are an important part of the story. You should aim to count at least ten broods, plus however many old birds you find in doing this. In the end you simply total up the numbers of young and old birds seen.

If there are any less than two young to each old bird, you will be wise to suspend shooting for the year in question. If you do shoot, you will probably be eating into next year's breeding stock. In good years there may be three or more young birds to each old one, in which case you should be able to shoot about 30 per cent of the population, but do not be tempted to overdo it. The Game Conservancy Trust's research shows that grey partridges should not be shot when the autumn population falls below 20 birds per square kilometre (250 acres). Real wild partridges at shootable levels are an asset to treasure. Treat them with respect, conserve them in every way possible and you should be able to enjoy some of the finest sport, and the finest gourmet dinners, that any sportsman can expect.

9

Woodcock

'Woodcock shooting is rough shooting of the finest type. It demands marksmanship and fieldcraft of a high order from the Gun, whether he is a shooting potterer
with a spaniel or bird dog, or walking-up as one of a line, or standing in a
semi-circle of guns as a covert is beaten out'

Colin McKelvie *The Book of the Woodcock* (1986)

Natural history and migration

The woodcock is very different from the two preceding species. Unlike them
it is migratory in habit, with the majority of our bag being made up of birds
bred overseas. Quite substantial numbers of woodcock do breed in the United
Kingdom, with only the westernmost fringes of the country lacking any home
breeders, but numbers there are heavily supplemented in winter from the
north and east.

While the woodcock is considered in legal terms as a gamebird, in some
senses at least, it would not be classified as such by most bird-watchers. By this,
I mean that it is not a member of the order *Galliformes*, which includes grouse,
pheasants, partridge and of course, the chicken. The woodcock is actually a
wader, of the same family as such familiar coastal birds as the curlew and
redshank. Like the classic waders, it uses its long bill to probe into soft ground
for food, but there the similarity ends. Instead of inhabiting the wide open
marshes, the woodcock spends much of its life in woods.

In summer it chooses woods as its nesting area, finding insects and worms
for food in the leaf litter that surrounds it, but in winter its habits change. At the
time when we are pursuing it, the woodcock feeds mainly on pastures, where
it probes for earthworms as its main diet. This is a night-time activity, with the
birds spending the day in quiet contemplation resting in the woods. Resting
sites do seem to vary a little, according to weather. On bright days in one of
my favourite areas, woodcock can often be found on sunny bracken banks,
but they rarely use them when it is really wet. Thick hedges are also chosen,

but again they seem to be less favoured on wet days. Woodland resting sites seem to conform to two characteristics. First they must be dry, even if the wood as a whole is wet. Secondly they must have easy access from above. Gaps in the woodland canopy are very much favoured.

Frost has an enormous effect on woodcock activity, and when the British Isles freeze up the birds move south and west in search of unfrozen ground. It can also have dramatic local effects too. There are places along streambeds in South Wales where you never see a woodcock in mild weather, but which are a certain find if it is really frosty. The woodcock which inhabit these places seem to feed all day long as well. I guess that these are really second-grade feeding areas, which are not worth bothering with when it is mild. However, when frost locks up the normal food supply, the woodcock move to such haunts, but then find that they have to feed almost continuously to obtain enough to keep them going.

I have often wondered whether these are woodcock which have been in the locality all winter, and have just changed their habits in response to frost, or whether they are newcomers. Whatever the truth, when these conditions prevail the woodcock population in the area concerned drops dramatically, so a fair proportion, at least, must move a considerable distance. There is one relevant radio-tracking study, carried out by The Game Conservancy Trust in Cornwall, in which a woodcock whose habits had been very regular all winter suddenly changed to a similar streambed station when the cold weather came.

As far as day-to-day habits are concerned, woodcock in their wintering areas seem remarkably regular. And yet, woodcock have the reputation in the sporting literature of being the most capricious of birds, here today and gone tomorrow. I suspect that this derives largely from observed characteristics in areas where they are really mainly passage migrants. Thus, at migration time in East Anglia, for example, you may find lots of newly-arrived woodcock one late autumn day, but a few days later there are very few. I believe that what happens is that a good number arrive together at the first landfall, having crossed the wide North Sea. Over the next few days they feed hard to regain some fat and then move on.

In normal weather, in their winter home, woodcock will often use the same resting place day after day. However, the birds will not put up with too much disturbance. Flush one today and you are quite likely to find the bird in the same place tomorrow, but if you keep disturbing him he will choose a quieter spot. Individual woodcock will normally go to the same feeding place each night too, using the same route to get there.

One of the most remarkable things about this, however, is that several other birds are also likely to use largely the same route. Thus, you find woodcock flightlines between resting areas and feeding fields. The odd thing is that the birds which use these fixed flightlines do not do so communally. They come out one at a time, with just the occasional couple, having spent their day widely

Wintering woodcock rest by day on the ground. *(Terence Blank)*

spread in the woods. I do not think they even feed communally either. My experience has been that, if you disturb woodcock at night, perhaps when lamping for rabbits, you move single birds from quite widely-spaced locations. This view is reinforced if you watch birds on a flightline. Two flightlines which I know particularly well lead off into the sunset, and if you watch the birds as they depart, they spread out into their feeding areas.

Woodcock are said to migrate mainly at the time of the full moon, with the one in October traditionally regarded as the 'woodcock moon' when the migrants arrive. In practice I have found this less than reliable. In my part of the south, home-bred woodcock seem to disappear in August and one rarely sees a bird until the migrants arrive. Whether they move off to the Continent, or simply become more elusive I do not know. Perhaps it is just that we do not hunt the woods much in autumn while the leaf is still on. However, my local flightlines are certainly uninhabited until the autumn migrants arrive. This does occur with the October moon, provided that it happens after the middle of the month. Otherwise the first real wave does not happen until November, although there are usually one or two birds about at the end of October whatever the state of the moon.

It seems to me that the first wave of migration is followed about a month later by a second and larger one. Certainly in the areas from Dorset to South Wales which I know well, our woodcock population seems to reach a peak in early December, unless hard weather causes a mass movement later in the winter. On the other hand, friends in East Anglia often report a good fall of woodcock as early as late October. Presumably, having made a landfall, the birds drift gently on to their chosen wintering area as the urge takes them.

A detailed account of the breeding biology of woodcock would be out of place here, but it is such a fascinating story that brief mention seems worthwhile. Most observant country people will have seen the roding display flight of a male woodcock at around sunset on a spring evening, but few will understand its real significance. What happens is that the local dominant male flies slowly around his territory producing a strange croaking noise, punctuated at regular intervals with a rather more far carrying squeak. This serves two functions: to assert his ownership, and to attract receptive females. If it is a 'prime' territory, it may well contain several females, each of which he will mate with over a period of time. It may well also contain several, usually young, subordinate males, who do not rode at all while the territory holder is in charge. However, if he dies, or remains in attendance with a female for a few days, one or another of the subordinates takes over. In the latter case the dominant bird returns in due course.

Woodcock nests are made on the ground, often at the base of a tree, and the female relies mainly on her 'dead leaf' camouflage to avoid predators rather than hiding in dense cover. A normal clutch, in common with most waders, is four eggs. These are surprisingly large and pale brown with darker reddish brown blotches.

The chicks are able to walk soon after hatching, and are led off in search of food by their mother. It is also clear that, at least occasionally, the adult bird will carry her young in flight. This is something which most people never see,

A carefully managed woodcock covert of the far west. The 'tunnel' ride is used at flight time. (*The Game Conservancy Trust*)

but those who have done so seem to agree that it is most often a response to crossing an impassable object such as a ditch or stream, rather than an attempt to avoid danger.

Woodcock shooting

Woodcock in winter are birds of the mild oceanic climes. Think of woodcock shooting and your thoughts will almost certainly turn to the Atlantic seaboard: West Cornwall, Pembrokeshire, Western Ireland, the Lleyn peninsula, and the Western Isles of Scotland have long been regarded as the places to go. Here, in the best areas, woodcock are the number one gamebird. Indeed there are still one or two driven woodcock shoots where the keepers' main job is to manage habitat for these fascinating little brown birds even though they hardly breed at all in these western outposts. Many people are apt to forget that far wider areas of Wales, the West Country, Ireland and Western Scotland have a generous complement of woodcock which come west each winter to enjoy the mild climate. However, while these areas provide a winter home for large numbers of woodcock, it has to be admitted that they rarely reach the high densities of the few 'best' spots.

Other areas too have their complement of woodcock, although in some places these are clearly mainly passage visitors rather than winter residents. A few unlucky parts of the country rarely see a woodcock at all, but most areas with some woodland will at least see the occasional bird. Usually however, the woodcock shooter will have to work hard for his sport. A brace will be what most Guns consider a good bag, and even in good areas blank days must be accepted as a serious possibility. A rare red-letter day might produce four or five to one Gun, and most shooters will never see the opportunity of a right and left. The woodcock is a distinctly solitary bird in winter, and you will rarely find two birds resting together.

If you are lucky enough to do so, and you succeed in shooting both to a 'proper' right and left, before two witnesses, you will qualify for membership of the *Shooting Times* Woodcock Club. The prize is a free subscription to *Shooting Times*, a special badge, and a bottle of Balvenie malt whisky. Only a 'proper' right and left qualifies. You must be aware that both birds are on the wing before you take the shot. If, as usually happens, you shoot the first and the second flushes 'on report', it does not qualify, and rightly so. If you get as excited as I have done on most occasions when two birds have shown together, you will fluff the first shot anyway.

Walking-up

Most woodcock shooters will pursue their sport by hunting-up their birds alone, or with one or two chosen companions. Where pheasants are the main quarry, woodcock will be largely considered as an incidental. However, in much of the wetter and hillier west, woodcock densities are high enough to become the main quarry. In these areas, thousands of years of human occupation has meant that most of the better and flatter land has gone over to agriculture. As a result, most of the remaining woods form long narrow strips on the steeper valley sides. Typically they are of oak, ash and birch, with willow and alder in the wetter places, and they often have a generous measure of holly bushes too, which can make favourite woodcock resting places.

These long, and often narrow, valley woods are ideally suited to being walked-up by small parties of rough shooters. Two or three Guns and a couple of thoroughly steady, close-working dogs are an ideal party.

Many people think that dogs are essential to show woodcock, but in fact a high proportion of birds will usually flush anyway provided the team of Guns are not too widely spaced. Dogs are therefore much more important for retrieving the bag than for showing them, and any that are inclined to range ahead are definitely bad news. Woodcock densities are rarely high, so it is frustrating in the extreme if most of them are flushed out of range by an over-enthusiastic dog. Even when they get up quite close by the odds are usually firmly on the woodcock rather than the Gun – woodcock have an uncanny knack of using the holly bush that they were resting under to screen their escape, and you are almost invariably tangled up in a thicket, or tripping over a boulder just as they clatter into the air. One keen woodcock shooter of south-west Wales estimated that only one in three of the woodcock flushed was likely to be shot at. He then felt that if he killed every third bird he was doing well – 9:1 odds in favour of the quarry.

There is something to be said for one of the pointing breeds here. The advantage of having the dog come on to point, and giving yourself time to get unravelled and ready for a shot is clear. The disadvantage is that in thicker cover, with the dog often out of sight, you may never know that it is on point anyway. Nevertheless, I gather that many continental woodcock shooters favour this method. In some cases they fit the dog with a falconer's bell, and when the bell stops ringing they know that the dog is on point. The second choice, and one also favoured for the slightly different American woodcock, is to use a Brittany spaniel, or other small hunt, point and retriever breed, which is trained to range a little wider than a close-working springer. The dog is therefore always in view, so you are not caught out when it comes on to point.

Many of the new woods in these hilly areas are in the form of single species conifer blocks. These are much more difficult to shoot successfully, but they do hold woodcock. This is especially so where the old farm fields have been planted up without touching the hedges. Over the years these grow up as a conifer block with a network of oak, thorn, holly and ash belts, often growing from a raised bank which form ideal woodcock resting sites. The bigger woods usually have at least some wide rides, but smaller blocks may well have no real access for the Gun. It can be possible to get a shot by hunting the edges or old hedgerows, but this is usually a pretty frustrating business. However, where rides are present, most of the woodcock seem to come into the wood by landing at the ride edge and walking into cover nearby. Guns who walk the rides, allowing their dogs to range for 30 to 40 yards on either side stand a good chance of flushing a few birds, and a surprising proportion will either cross the ride or choose to fly along it.

Clearings in larger woods are the other main sites which woodcock choose for resting. In fact the birds rarely sit in the clearing. They alight in it and then walk off into cover. Thus, as noted with the pheasant, the wise woodcock shooter faced with an enormous block of wood will study it carefully, find the hot spots along the edges, along ride sides, and near clearings, and plan his attack to cover these in logical sequence.

Small drives

As with most other walked-up game, there comes a time in hunting woodcock when it is best for a party to split up and attempt to show birds to one another. Woodcock are far from easy to drive. They will rarely face a long flight in open country, and they will often fly out through the trees rather than climbing above them, so high-driven birds are not easy to achieve. Also, they often have a habit of going where they choose, rather than where you want to drive them. All this means that lines of Guns in the fashion of a formal pheasant shoot are liable to be rather a waste of time. A much better option is to study your birds and your ground, and to place standing Guns on favoured escape routes, such as tall hedges and narrow belts.

Do not attempt too long a drive for woodcock. Birds will often go forward when first flushed, but then break back, and they rarely go more than 200 or 300 yards. Indeed, a wise policy, especially on woods which get narrower as one goes up a valley, is to start off with the full team walking, and then drop off a couple of Guns half-way up to intercept birds breaking back. Another variation comes where there is a thicket in which it is rarely possible to take a shot. The main party surrounds the thicket, and one member crashes through as best he can, hopefully with a couple of dogs working around him to help flush the birds. In this way birds which might never offer a shot to the lone rough shooter can provide good sport.

Flighting

Another approach to birds which rarely offer a shot, either because they inhabit very thick cover or because they are widely spread over a large and difficult wood, is to locate the flightlines and shoot them there. As mentioned earlier, woodcock from quite large areas will often choose a relatively narrow flight-line to and from their roosting and feeding areas. Location of flightlines is far from easy, and you will have to be prepared to wait at dusk or dawn at selected vantage points and watch what goes on. Woodcock flight in marginally better light conditions than duck, which is just as well, because they would be almost impossible to see in the woods at deepest dusk. Birds tend to emerge through the treetops in conifer woods, and between the trunks of mature trees, dipping down and skimming low over the ground as soon as they emerge, so you will often have to be almost on the flightline before you discover it. Some examples may help:

The first flightline which I ever knew was shown to me by one of the keenest woodcock shots of South Wales. It follows a gentle dip up the side of a steep wooded valley, which in turn forms part of a larger forestry complex, and up to 25 woodcock come out over a front not more than 70 yards wide, most following a tall hedge which forms the continuation of the dip. They then spread out to feed on the rich pastures of the relatively flat hilltop.

Another flightline comes out between two hedges perhaps 150 yards apart, at the edge of a forestry block, where it is bounded by four or five particularly rich pastures, used to provide silage and grazing for a dairy herd. There is yet another, though less popular, flightline (it is only used by four or five birds) out of the opposite side of this wood, where again there are a couple of rich fields. The rest of the wood is surrounded by dry sheep pastures, unimproved boggy fields and wet heath, which presumably produce far less food.

The fourth flightline follows a small alder-lined stream where it enters a huge block of forestry. Again it leads to rich pastures, grazed mainly by cattle and horses, but not sheep. The last example is in chalk country and follows a wide ride out of a large wood. It is in an area of fairly low woodcock density and I have never seen more than six woodcock using it. The surrounding country is all chalk downland and arable fields, and I have no idea exactly where the woodcock go to feed. They go out along exactly the same route as they use to return at dawn, a feature which is not common to all flightlines.

These five flightlines, then, offer some of the most exciting shooting I know. How many birds will come is never certain, and sport can be fast and furious. Also, it is snap shooting *par excellence*. The birds appear for a split second through the treetops before dipping below the skyline out of sight, so you must position yourself in shot of where you expect them to appear, and shoot quickly. Occasionally a bird comes high and very fast – I assume it is a longer distance traveller. As you mount your gun, you realise that it is not following a straight course at all, but zigzagging like a snipe. I nearly always miss these.

Some opinion rather frowns on flight shooting as unsporting, but I really do feel that it provides testing sport, with a far wider variety of shots than those experienced at driven shoots. As proof of how demanding it can be, I offer the example of one particular line in Wales, which I have shot once or twice a season for the last seven or eight years. We usually see between five and ten birds, and on average I seem to get shots at three or four. Now I can only remember shooting two birds on this line in all those years, and I am not *that* bad a shot really. My chum who shoots it with me has recorded similar 'success'.

In country where woodcock can be shot during the day by walking-up, shooting flightlines is probably being greedy. You can hardly expect a wild resource like this to stand being worked twice. However, where there are large forestry blocks, or similar impossible cover, flightlines may be the only opportunity, and I see no harm in taking it.

A word of warning should be sounded however, Woodcock flightlines are the most easily over-shot resource I know. I have yet to find one flightline that will stand more than two goes in a season, *even if you miss all the birds both times.*

A woodcock comes lazily out, and you miss with both barrels, but he seems to fly on unperturbed. There may be a twist of avoidance, but there is none of the sudden acceleration shown by pigeons or wildfowl. However, if you wait on your flightline the following evening you will find that far fewer birds emerge. It seems to take several weeks for woodcock to regain their confidence. My normal procedure therefore, is to go once early in the season, just after the main arrival, and then to rest things for at least a month before having a second go. I have tried for the third session more than once, always with the same result – a poor showing. Also, things were less than satisfactory in the following season in all cases. If you have a flightline on your shoot, treasure it as the sporting jewel it is, and treat it with respect. Remember also that it is illegal to shoot game during the period from one hour after sunset to one hour before sunrise. Woodcock are wonderful birds, and all the indications are that they are on the increase. Please do not abuse them.

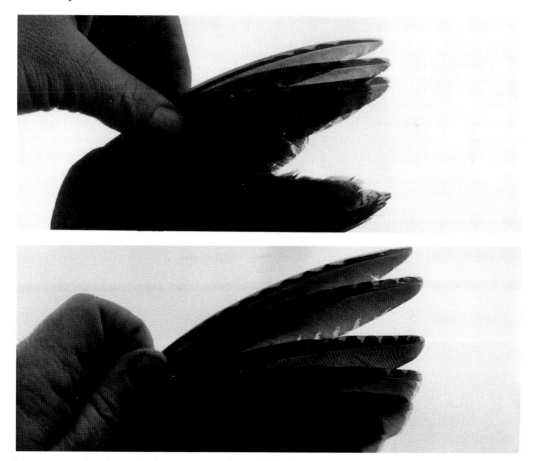

Young woodcock are far better to eat than old birds. Look for frayed tips to the two outer-most wing feathers as above. Smooth feathers (below) indicate an old bird.

10

Snipe

'Successful snipe-shooting seems to me in the final analysis to depend on slick, incisive, polished gun mounting more than in the pursuit of any other quarry.'

Roderick Willett *Modern Game Shooting* (1975)

Natural history and migration

The snipe is one of my favourite birds. A small skittish bundle of energy, it seems to lead life at breakneck speed. No other bird zips off so smartly when flushed, and no other seems to take quite the same headlong dive to ground. You feel that it will surely hit the earth so hard that it is bound not only to commit suicide, but also to bury itself, and then, only a foot or two above the ground, the air-brakes go on and it alights as light as a feather. Some of my

A snipe bog of the far west. Note the small patches of open water – a key feature in attracting snipe. *(The Game Conservancy Trust)*

A remarkably tame snipe in a watercress bed. *(Hugo Straker, The Game Conservancy Trust)*

happiest sporting memories are of hunting the bogs and ditches, and many a blank morning flight on the coast has been saved by walking the high marsh for snipe later on.

Snipe are quite closely related to woodcock, but they are birds of the marsh and not woodland. Nevertheless, in frosty weather you may well flush snipe from unfrozen patches under trees, or in areas of wet willow scrub. At the other end of the scale, I have found them in a number of strange places. I know of corn stubbles on chalk downland which are regularly visited by snipe on autumn passage. I have flushed them on dry heathland, and I have even shot one when walking a strawberry field for partridges, on the Gower peninsula in South Wales. These all are, however, the exceptions that prove the rule. Snipe are really birds of bogs, ditch and pond-sides, wet rushy pastures and the like.

Like the woodcock, they are migratory, and the majority of our winter population comes from overseas. Even so, large numbers do breed on our marshes and moors, and home-bred birds can often be found at the start of their season 'the Glorious Twelfth' (the first day of September in Ireland). Snipe migration also appears to be in waves, but there seems less of a tie to the phases of the moon. Also, the first migrants clearly occur much earlier in the autumn, and good numbers can often be found in the wintering grounds as early as mid-October, long before any but the first woodcock have arrived.

Unlike woodcock, wintering snipe do not have such a rigid daily rhythm of roosting and feeding. They seem to feed at all hours of the day or night, and are far less likely to move from feeding to roosting places. However, there is still a tendency to flight at dawn and dusk, so presumably some feeding grounds are only considered safe under cover of darkness.

Like woodcock, snipe are ground nesters, with a similar characteristic clutch of four eggs. However, they seem to form normal pair bonds like most other birds, and some authorities suggest that the male helps with rearing the young once they hatch.

Snipe can be very variable in their 'jumpiness'. Some birds sit so tight that you almost tread on them before they flush, and others are off before you have approached within 100 yards. There does not seem to be much logic in what happens either, except that some days they seem more jumpy than others, and they certainly seem inclined to sit tighter in frosty weather. Also, the larger the group the more jumpy they are. Singles often sit quite tight, but a group of a dozen will be off together well beyond gunshot. However, if you flush a group, do not despair, there is often a laggard who sits tight after the rest have left. Do beware, however, if a snipe jumps up under your feet without the usual 'scaap' call and goes off dead straight offering an easy shot; it is probably a jack snipe, and these are now protected in the United Kingdom. These smallest snipe are much more common than most bird-watchers think; it is just that they sit tight and are rarely seen by anyone except those who actively hunt the bogs. When the snipe erupts into the air, with its 'scaap' call which almost sounds like the squelch of the bog, it does so with a wondrously deceptive zigzag, and is far from easy to hit.

Snipe shooting

The majority of snipe are probably shot as incidentals to other game, or as part of mixed days. Few people have a large area of snipe ground at their disposal, but for many shoots walking a couple of boggy meadows adds variety to a day. It is thus probably fair to say that nine out of ten of the snipe that are shot are walked-up rather than driven.

Walking-up

Much has been written over the years about the best way to walk a snipe bog, with wind direction generally considered a governing factor. Some opinion has suggested that you walk with the wind, and that the snipe, in rising into the wind (as all birds do), will be coming towards you. If they then continue to come you almost have a driven shot, and if they turn to go down on the wind, you are offered a good shot as the turn commences.

The trouble with this system is that the wind carries the noise of your approach, and I have found that a larger proportion of the birds rise out of shot, before turning and flying off downwind. I have never found that they keep coming rather than turning in sufficient numbers to warrant using this technique if there is a choice.

Walking into the wind undoubtedly allows a closer approach, and a greater proportion of birds rise in shot. However, I prefer a variation if I can manage it, which is to walk across the wind. This results in birds which rise into the wind offering crossing shots, and irons out most of the zigzag of the initial rise since this is now simply towards and away from the Gun. Also, I find that a crosswind approach seems to allow as close an approach as walking upwind.

All of this discussion may well be largely academic anyway, as you find either that it is a flat calm day, or that your approach is governed by the lie of the land. So often snipe are found along a ditch side, or in some other linear habitat in which you are forced to walk in one of two directions. An example of this is given by one of my favourite bogs in Wales. This is roughly triangular in shape, and surrounded on two sides by the houses of a village, so one can really only walk it away from the houses whatever the wind.

Another question which has often been debated is *when* to shoot. Most authorities have suggested that you shoot the moment the bird rises, before it has the chance to start its deceptive zigzag flight, but a few have offered an alternative – namely, that you wait until the bird stops zigzagging and straightens out. My own experience is that the zigzag usually carries on for a good 30 yards or more before the bird straightens out and starts a fairly steep climb. In practice, if you wait, even a bird which rose at your feet would be out of shot before it straightened out. I find that at least half of my birds rise out of shot, so any fair offer is a candidate for instant action. However, do beware the bird which rises at the limit of range. If you shoot you are most likely to drive off any other birds within 100 yards. If you are confident that there will only be this one offer, get on with it, but if your ground normally harbours a few birds, it may be best to allow the marginals to pass in the hope of a better chance later. It is a case of balancing a chance of 'a bird in the hand' against the very real possibility of 'two in the bush'.

Which brings me to the question of dogs on the snipe bog. There is no no doubt in my mind that a hunting dog is a mixed blessing. It may flush birds that you would not have moved, but you risk moving birds early that might otherwise have shown in range. Also, since snipe so often go off low, you are bound to have to pass up some shots for the safety of the dog. I therefore prefer to keep my old retriever at heel. She simply serves the very valuable function of helping me to find shot birds. However, I do not send her straight away, but walk to the fall, so that if another bird flushes, I can take another shot. This would, incidentally, be very risky without a dog, since I have learned the hard way that in shooting a second bird I often forgot my mark on the first. Good dogs can accurately mark four or five birds, but most shooters do well to get two.

If I was hunting snipe on the great bogs of Ireland and Scotland my opinion of dogs on the snipe bog might well change. So many of these areas have but a thin population of snipe, and you could walk all day for hardly a shot. However, if you have the assistance of a good, wide-ranging but steady, setter or pointer you can cover so much more ground and improve your sport out of all proportion. I even have a friend who uses a pointing dog in this way on the wide valley bogs of the New Forest.

Driving

There is no doubt in my mind that where snipe are thinly spread in ones and twos, walking-up gives the best opportunities. However, as I mentioned earlier, it is a basic truth that larger groups of snipe are often more jumpy. Add to this the fact that your first shot flushes most of the birds left in the bog, and it becomes clear that walking-up groups can be a very frustrating business. Given these problems, it can pay handsomely to consider driving whenever you are not alone, and there is cover to hide behind. I have had some very successful drives when shooting with just one companion, and there is no doubt at all that when the party is larger than this, you are much more likely to get some shooting for everyone if you place the majority of Guns in sensible positions and get just one or two to walk the ground over them.

Wind is even more important when driving, however, and snipe will often stalwartly refuse to go in your chosen direction if it does not suit them. In areas where there are plenty of bogs, any escape direction will provide a haven, and you must pay attention to wind if you want to get any real degree of success. Snipe driven across the wind will go off in all sorts of directions, and the standard practice is to drive them into the wind. However, I have found that driving with the wind works too. This has the advantage that the noise of the standing team getting into position is carried away from the birds, but even so, everyone must get to his stand as quietly and as invisibly as possible. Downwind driving does tend to result in something of a spread of birds, but in a strong blow they can be onto the Guns almost before they have had a

A snipe feeding area alongside a rutted track. Note the probe marks. *(The Game Conservancy Trust)*

chance to sort themselves out. The advantage of upwind driving is that it is often rather more directional, and that the birds will often fly low, to avoid the brunt of the wind for some distance. However, when they do climb it can be very rapid, and they are soon at the limit of range. In practice, they key to success is to get everyone into place as quietly as possible, and to try to get them as near as possible to the bulk of the birds.

If your country has but few areas of snipe habitat, you will soon notice a tendency for birds to head off towards the next nearest suitable place, rather than fanning out in all directions. In this case wind direction can be largely forgotten in placing your Guns, although it may still have its effect on the initial departure direction. I have also found that it helps, when running a snipe drive, to get the walking Guns to fire the first shots. This seems to encourage the birds forward over the standing Guns.

A variation on the driving technique which can work well is to drive or walk your best bog at the start of the day, and then to leave a Gun or two hidden near the favourite places on it. You then go off and work the subsidiary bogs, and the birds which are flushed here will tend to return to the main bog. Your hidden Guns get some amazingly testing shots at snipe which literally dive-bomb them on their return. You meanwhile get good sport walking-up these places, where the birds, which are now split into smaller groups, tend to sit tighter. They thus offer more sport than they did on the main bog, where they probably rose wild and *en masse*.

Flighting

I do not know of any rigid flightlines like those of the woodcock, but snipe do tend to move around at dawn and dusk. This gives two possibilities for sport. One is to intercept them on passage, and the other is to wait at their point of arrival. I know of one gap in the hills in Wales which seems to act as a focus for snipe at dusk, but I have never really worked out where they are going to. However, it has given me a shot or two over the years, when waiting for the woodcock to flight. I also know a couple of places where a snipe or two come to the side of the pool at dusk, a little before duck flight time. Again, they would hardly be worth the wait on their own, but they are a good incentive to be a little early for the evening flight of duck.

I also suspect that the snipe in some of the denser populations which I know of probably fan out into odd small feeding stations by night, and return to their main marsh at dawn, but I have never been well enough organised to be there at dawn flight time, when the lure of the foreshore or a woodcock flight has been stronger.

Shot sizes

As mentioned earlier, snipe are one of the few quarry species for which I depart from my normal choice of 28g (1oz) of No.7 shot as the preferred load. Given the choice, I like 8s every time, and my greatest successes were with Eley's (now defunct) paper-cased Trapshooting 8s in the mid-1970s. For a while, 8s were almost impossible to find, but I now see several manufacturers again offering clay cartridges loaded with 8s. If only they would go back to fibre or felt wads so that we did not have to spread plastic litter on the bogs. In the absence of 8s, 7s will do, but I think I prefer skeet loads of 9s. My good friend Colin McKelvie tells me that there is a strong contingent of Irish snipe shooters who use 25in barrelled 12-bore shotguns, with no choke, and skeet loads of 9s as their standard equipment. Such a choice makes a lot of sense if snipe are your main quarry, but you should not be tempted by larger quarry such as rabbits or hares unless they are very close.

While it remains legal to shoot snipe with lead, some snipe shooting is carried out over wetlands where there is a statutory ban on the use of lead shot. Also, compliance with the Code of Good Shooting Practice means that responsible shooters will wish to avoid depositing lead pellets in wetlands of significance to feeding waterfowl. With suitable small non toxic shot hard to find, my best compromise has been to use bismuth 7s in these circumstances.

11
Ground Game

'In shooting them, think only of the head; there is no question of aiming, as there must be with a high pheasant: you swing your gun at them, thinking only of the head, and, shot through the head, the rabbit turns somersaults.'

Eric Parker *Elements of Shooting* (1924)

The humble bunny

What is the rabbit to you? For many rough shooters, the rabbit is the essence of their sport in the countryside, but they should remember that the rabbit is also a serious agricultural pest. The damage caused to farming by rabbits preserved for shooting reached such a pitch in the last century, that the Ground Game Act was passed by Parliament in 1871. This gave, and continues to give, all farmers the inalienable right to control their own rabbits, or to employ someone to do it for them. Interestingly, it is clear that the Act did lead some tenants to give up farming and simply crop rabbits – a situation which is no longer economic.

Thus, if you rent a shoot from a farmer, he retains the right to control the rabbits on it. He might give a verbal agreement not to, but this has no legal foundation. A more complex situation arises when you rent shooting over land which has a tenant farmer. Again, the farmer can control rabbits – and you cannot expect him to leave them alone. So, do not take shooting purely for bunnies, and do consult with the farmer over the damage which they might do and how you can help to prevent it. More shoot relations have been spoiled over the humble rabbit than over any other quarry, so do be careful how you approach the situation.

The rabbit is an introduced species in the British Isles. It was almost certainly brought over by the Romans, who kept rabbits for food, the particular delicacy being the part-grown foetus, and not the adult. Basically a grazing animal, which normally lives in underground burrows (warrens), the rabbit will however, take a very wide range of foods, according to what is available. Thus, for example, when the world is white with hard frozen snow, and the grass locked out of reach, rabbits will take to eating the bark of trees and bushes, causing enormous damage in so doing. The rabbit's legendary liking for carrots is not entirely unfounded either, as is proven by the recently developed cage-trapping techniques using carrots as bait. The main damage as far as the farmer is concerned, however, is to growing crops of corn, grass, fodder and perhaps most expensive of all, horticultural cash crops.

Rabbits will often live above ground in bushes, scrub and other cover, especially outside the main breeding season. This is a great help to the rough shooter, who might otherwise rarely get a shot at a bunny except by stalking the odd ones sitting out at evening time. I mention 'main breeding season' because rabbits have been known to produce young in all months of the year. Most adult does will have several litters each year, normally in the period January to June. However, the expression 'breed like rabbits' is distinctly unfair, since rabbits can exercise very efficient birth control. In very high population densities, with food hard to find, rabbits produce very few young. Those does who do get pregnant do not normally complete their full term. The embryos are resorbed back into the body of the doe. However, with a low to medium population, and abundant food, rabbits do breed fast, and early-born does will have their first litters in the same year as they themselves were born. Hence the speed with which rabbits are able to rebuild their population after a concentrated control campaign.

The young are normally born underground, in a simple blind stop, away from the burrow network of the warren. They usually number four or five to a litter, but up to seven or eight are possible. They are born blind and hairless, and are unable to leave the burrow until they are about 4 weeks old; by 6 weeks they become largely independent, while their mother makes preparations for her next litter. Females are normally mated again within a few days of birth, and the new litter is produced 8 weeks later.

Since the first arrival of myxomatosis in the mid-1950s the British rabbit population has been severely affected. This killer disease, which results in lesions around the eyes and ears and rapid loss of condition, is caused by a virus which is spread by blood parasites. In some countries, mosquitos are a vector, but in the United Kingdom the infective agent is carried by the rabbit flea. When the disease first appeared it is calculated to have killed about 99.6 per cent of the United Kingdom rabbit population. Of the remaining 0.4 per cent, about half were believed to have escaped infection and the other half to have survived it. Over the subsequent four and a half decades, the virulence of myxomatosis has declined, and genetic resistance in the population has increased, so that rabbits are once more a very common animal. In many populations there is an outbreak in the early autumn, when the new crop of young become infected. Some die and some survive to remain immune for the rest of their lives.

Most people dispose of any infected rabbits which they catch or shoot, but there is no evidence that eating infected animals is harmful. Myxomatosis has never been recorded in any other British wildlife except in a very few hares, and the likes of foxes and buzzards must regularly eat diseased rabbits raw. However, loss of condition once symptoms show is so rapid, that any infected bunnies would without doubt make poor eating.

Over the last ten years a new disease has hit rabbits, viral haemorrhagic disease (VHD), which is reputed to have caused some local problems. VHD does not appear to have been anything like as dramatic as myxomatosis was in the 1950s.

The leaping hare

Unlike the rabbit, the hare, or should I say hares, are believed to be native to the British Isles. We have two species, the brown hare of the lowlands of England, Wales and Scotland, and the mountain or blue hare of the northern uplands and Ireland. There is now some evidence that the brown hare may have been introduced by the Romans, but it never managed to colonise the Emerald Isle, its place in the lowlands of Ireland being taken by the mountain species.

The brown hare retains its brown coat all year round, but the mountain hares of northern Britain are greyer and turn white in winter, to match the snow of the high hills. The Irish version is intermediate being redder in colour than the mountain hare, and going partially white in winter. The brown hare is also the largest of the two, averaging perhaps 3.6kg (8lb) in weight, while the mountain is smaller, around 2.7kg (6lb). A white hare is obviously easy to tell from a rabbit, but young hares are quite similar to look at and may cause confusion. However, both hare species are leggier, faster and have longer ears which have black tips.

The Hare is a master of the quick turn – and far too easy to miss. *(Terence Blank)*

The two species are very similar in both ecology and breeding system. Unlike rabbits they do not burrow. They do, however, rest in a seat or hollow in the vegetation which is known as a form. An individual hare will normally have a number of these within its home range, and will use whichever is suitable to the circumstances in which it finds itself.

Just like rabbits, hares are primarily grazers, but again shortage of food will lead to bark stripping and eating of young trees and bushes, especially the latter when they are the only things visible above the snow. Hare damage rarely reaches the levels achieved by rabbits, but can nonetheless be a real problem. However, they do not much like to share their fields with high densities of livestock, so damage usually ceases when a farmer moves his stock into hare feeding grounds.

Unlike rabbits, the hare young (leverets) are born above ground. Although born in a group of up to four or five, they soon separate and hide singly. They then gather together when the doe visits to suckle, otherwise remaining quite still in their individual forms.

Unlike bunnies, hares are born with open eyes, are able to walk from birth and have a full coat of hair. These tiny leverets, often hidden in the most exposed of places, are very vulnerable to predation – hence their spacing. They also suffer from well-meaning people who assume that they are abandoned and 'rescue' them. If you find a leveret immobile in its form, leave well alone and do not come back to check on it every five minutes. Given some peace, mother will return and move it to a new form once the danger of your presence has passed.

Shooting rabbits and hares

Many shoots have a rule against shooting ground game – and very sensible it can be. Send a few Guns, a couple of beaters, and a team of dogs into a thicket, and if you take shots at ground level the dangers can be enormous. Remember that the odd pellet can go off at a tangent in the first place and then perhaps ricochet if it strikes a stone or branch. Shooting ground game in company is a risky business and needs tight safety rules. On balance, I really do think that the no ground game rule has a lot going for it when the prime aim is the likes of pheasants or woodcock.

Many Guns also refuse to shoot hares. There are three main reasons for this. One is that a wounded hare has a blood-curdling and rather human sounding scream which so upsets some people that they cannot bring themselves to shoot them. The second is that hares have been in decline due to intensification of farming over the last three decades. The third is that formal hare shoots can be very unattractive. Invitations to very inexperienced Guns are not uncommon, and a combination of unsafe shooting, and shots taken at excessive range is all too frequent. Well-organised hare drives do a good job in hare control, and can be a pleasure to participate in. Badly-organised ones are a nightmare.

Rough cover and bunnies

Rough gorse banks, patches of brambles, areas of bracken or rush, thick hedgerows and reed-fringed ditches can all harbour rabbits that sit out in cover rather than hiding underground. Such ground can provide tremendous sport as you hunt-up, and the rabbits race to the next patch of cover, jinking and twisting like snipe all the way. This is walked-up shooting *par excellence*, provided that your dog does not run-in. There is no doubt that rabbiting like this is the greatest test of dog training. Any dog which is steady to the bolt of a bunny from under its nose, and then drops to shot every time can really be said to be steady. The only greater temptation which I know is to join the chase after a hare when other dogs go off in hot pursuit.

From the moment of flush, a rabbit makes ground at an amazing rate. Anything that bolts at 30 yards is almost bound to be out of shot before you have got your gun mounted, so you really do need a close-working dog for this kind of sport. If you are working a patch of rough ground, you will do well to limit your dog to 10 yards either side of you, and no more than 5 yards in front. In this way you cover a 20 yard wide band efficiently. Allowing a wider range means both missed chances, because rabbits bolt out of range, and inefficient work, which does not shift them all anyway. A close-working dog also allows you time to pick your shots without risk to the dog who will be almost under your feet when the rabbit bolts.

Wherever possible, you should aim to work upwind, as this helps your dog to find the game. It also means that both the noise of your approach, and your scent, are blown away from the quarry. Given a wide patch of cover, you will need to plan a strategy to cover it strip by strip. The choice is between working successive strips upwind and the next down, or doing a crosswind zigzag. In the end I favour the latter as the best compromise, but you will often find the intimate knowledge of the ground and features of geography overrule fixed strategies, and that you work a sequence of cover going from one hot spot to another and working gradually upwind.

Hedges or other narrow strips are again best worked upwind if possible. Here it is best to have two Guns if you can, as most hedges are too high to allow you to shoot those rabbits which bolt on the other side. If you are alone, I suggest that you choose the side with the highest crop, or nearest alternative cover as giving the best chances. Unlike pheasants, rabbits rarely run on far ahead of the Guns, so teams of three or more Guns are better to stick together, with perhaps one in the cover and one each side if it is not too thick, or two on the best side with the outer Gun a little ahead and 10 yards into the field.

Patches of scrub and bramble over head height can be hotching with rabbits but distinctly difficult to shoot. You can stalk round quietly in the evenings or early mornings and hope to surprise a few, but otherwise they are difficult to shoot alone. One friend, however, had a system which worked beautifully. He had a Jack Russell terrier, which was trained to run out to the far side of the clump, like a collie working sheep, and then hunt it back to him. All he had to do was walk quietly into position on the downwind side and send the dog. I am sure that any other dog could be trained to the same technique.

Walked-up hares

Hares can be walked-up from rough cover in exactly the same way as rabbits, but I have a feeling that they sit less tight, and that dogs often do little to help. Where they are widely spaced, however, they will often hold to a pointing dog, so hare shooting over setters or pointers is a distinct possibility.

Hares will often sit out in open ground – especially winter corn, stubbles and moorland edges. In these circumstances they will often bolt at 20 yards or more so dogs at heel are much the best plan. Two hares in the bag are a heavy burden for the rest of a long walked-up day. Personally, I am so fond of roast saddle and jugged hare that I will shoot one if allowed, but I limit my bag to just one for the pot.

Driving

Time was when it was well-known practice to 'stink out' rabbit burrows. Rags were soaked in any one of a number of noxious (and now largely illegal) substances and pushed into the burrows. The woods were then driven with teams of beaters to standing Guns, and enormous numbers of rabbits shot. Such driving is largely gone today, although the return of more rabbits to almost pre-myxomatosis levels may make it a possibility again.

However, rabbit driving on a smaller scale is far from redundant. The system with the Jack Russell terrier described earlier is, after all, driving. Given two Guns in the party, it is simplicity itself to take turns to stand while the other man pushes out the thicket and sends the bunnies forward. Larger parties can arrange their division to suit the cover and the likely directions of escape. A Gun left standing back is a likely ruse too, especially if some of the rabbits in the clump have just been driven into it from a previous patch.

In more wooded situations, it can be well worthwhile to stand a Gun or two on the woodland rides, while others bring the cover through. This system works well in larger woods, but it is important to not take in too large a patch. Rabbits will rarely want to travel more than about 100 yards, so short drives are the order of the day.

For hares, on the other hand, there is much less reluctance to move over long distances, or to face open ground. Also, hares spend some of their time in woods, especially in cold weather. Hare drives should therefore take in larger areas including fields and woods. However, it is unwise to try to take in too large a patch for the size of your party. Aside from the fact that hares will escape to the sides if the party is too widely spaced, there is the temptation to take long shots rather than waste a chance. This is always unsporting whatever the quarry, but wounded hare is particularly difficult to retrieve since it travels so far. Also, since it is on the ground rather than flying, you are liable to lose sight of where it is going.

Standing Guns for rabbits or hares should be placed at the downwind side of the covert being driven. They should get into place quietly and *stand still*. A hare or rabbit sees movement quickly, but cannot really focus on distant forms. Those who keep still and quiet will get more than their share of the shooting and have less need to pull on fleeting glimpses, thereby reducing the risk of wounding.

Over ferrets

Rabbiting with ferrets is really outside the scope of this book, and I therefore only mention it in passing. If you choose to keep ferrets and work rabbits, you will probably choose mainly the quiet option of netting the burrows. This has the dual advantage of producing top quality, unshot rabbits for the pot or market, and not disturbing other game unduly. Many farmers and keepers will be delighted to allow honest reliable people as much ferreting as they want provided that no guns are involved.

Discussion of ferret management is really inappropriate here, but I would enter one plea. Too many ferrets are kept in diabolical conditions. Given good sound hutches, good fresh food, water and proper management they are clean

Just pop in the ferret, load up and stand back. Bolting rabbits are ripping sport. *(John Marchington)*

and friendly animals which are an enormous pleasure to own. Shut in a dark smelly shed with no opportunity to stay clean, and fed a rubbish diet like bread and milk, they are evil smelling and often spiteful. Please do look after your ferrets properly, supply a healthy diet, and remove leftover food daily, before it begins to rot.

Where rabbits are burrowing in open ground, shooting over ferrets is ripping sport. Done carefully it is also the system which results in least 'lie-ups'. Rabbit and ferret are sworn enemies, and the instinctive response of a rabbit when a ferret arrives in the burrow is to get out fast. However, given heavy human footfalls overhead, the rabbit is less sure, and may well decide to settle for hiding in a blind burrow down below.

Setting nets over a warren without alerting the rabbits is difficult, but if you creep quietly up from downwind, pop your ferret in, and settle quietly a few yards back, there is less risk of rabbits sitting tight. You wait quietly for the rabbits to bolt, shoot what comes, gather up your ferret, and move on to the next burrow.

Two important rules need to be added. The first is to feed your ferret a light breakfast before you start. Good ferrets hunt for fun, and the old wives' tale that they need to be half starved to work is nonsense. A hungry ferret is much more likely to kill below ground, gorge itself, and then go to sleep for the rest of the day, which leaves you with a lot of spade work or waiting if you want to carry on. The second rule is never shoot a rabbit until it is well clear of its burrow. Too many rabbits sitting in the entrance have a ferret attached to their scut, and I have more than once heard tales of woe from friends who have shot their best ferret.

Excessive use of modern gadgets is frowned upon in most sports, and ferreting is no exception. Purists are much against the use of radio collars or ferret locaters, saying that it makes the sport too easy. Personally, when out with a gun, I like to use one. If my ferret lies up, I have to dig but a single hole to find it, and my reward is usually a clean rabbit too. This I do not mind, but use of 'liners' and multiple excavations is no part of a day's shooting in my view. Nor is patient waiting for the ferret to emerge after a big feed and a long sleep.

Shot sizes and safety

It may seem odd to link shot size and safety – however, there is an important point here. No. 7 shot will kill rabbits very well, and hares too, at reasonable ranges but there is no doubt that larger sizes would be better for hares. The problem is that as shot size, and therefore striking energy, increases, so does the tendency to ricochet. I have seen people with wildfowling loads of 1s and even BB for hare driving, and this is patently not necessary. It increases the temptation to take long shots, results in more wounded beasts, and adds greater risks for other people and their dogs. Personally, I leave my dogs at home when out after hares in company. I know that they are safe, and that there is no risk of them running in and embarrassing me. As to shot sizes, I have never felt underpowered with game loads of 5s or even 6s, and have killed hares very cleanly when after snipe and loaded with 8s. However, 20 yards is quite far enough under such circumstances.

Woodcock have a reputation for tempting people to take dangerous shots, but my experience is that bolting bunnies in broken cover cause more excitement than any other game. Do please always be ultra careful. *Remember*: 'Never, never let your gun . . .'; 'Follow not across the line'; 'Never shoot where you can't see'. If everyone followed this advice, shooting accidents would not happen.

12
Wildfowl

'. . . and there are always duck coming in after we have gone – which is the secret of its success. The lead-in is never destroyed.'

Alan Savory *Lazy Rivers* (1956)

Wildfowling is a sport in itself, many would say the most exhilarating shooting sport, and books much larger than this one have been dedicated to wildfowling alone. Summarising all that has been written before into my one chapter would be impossible, and anyway, much of it is outside the scope of this book.

What I hope to do is to give a little guidance on the ways in which the rough

Pinkfeet and 'several' of them, over the moss in Lancashire. *(Ian Grindy)*

shooter can make the best of those wildfowl which visit his ground. For most people this will mean getting to grips with the occasional mallard which comes to a pond somewhere, but there are many other possibilities too.

Migration patterns

There are nine species of legal quarry duck, and four species of goose (see Chapter 6). With the exception of the introduced Canada goose, wildfowl of the British Isles are largely migratory, although most species breed here too. It is nevertheless true to say that the wildfowling season does not really get under way until the winter migrants arrive. September wildfowling is made up largely of the pursuit of home-bred mallard.

Migration patterns vary enormously from species to species. Thus, for example, the majority of our wintering pinkfoot geese arrive, *en masse*, in late September, none having bred in the British Isles. Teal, on the other hand, come and go with enormous unpredictability. A few breed with us, and the first overseas migrants will have joined these by the start of the season on 1 September. Waves of migrants will then come and go through the autumn, and marshes which were full in early October may well be deserted for the rest of the season. This will often vary too, from year to year.

To take another example, Siberian whitefronted geese usually arrive late with some haunts deserted until almost Christmas. Hard weather in January can bring an enormous influx of wildfowl from the near Continent – particularly to southern Britain. However, if the frost persists, it may well drive the birds further south and west. Heavy rains and flooding can have an enormous effect too, with many coastal birds moving inland.

Duck on the move at dusk. You may not even realise that they visit your shoot unless you know the signs.

It is thus clear that the possibilities for the rough shooter will vary on an almost daily basis throughout the season. Those who have their eyes open will spot what is going on, and will be able to reap the reward. In wildfowling, more than in any other shooting sport, there is no substitute for active study of the birds. Those people who do not take steps to find out what their wildfowl are doing can only expect the occasional chance shot. There are some basic rules which will help you to predict likely activity on a day-to-day basis, but, these are not hard and fast, so 'the best laid plans of mice and men . . .'

Flighting patterns

Geese are basically daylight feeders. Under normal circumstances they will spend the night at roost on some wide open safe haven. Typical examples are large lakes, estuaries, sandbanks or even the open sea. Sometime between dawn and sunrise, depending on the species, they fly off to their feeding ground. These again vary, according to the species to some extent. This rhythm does tend to break down at the time of the full moon, when the birds may well feel quite safe on the feeding grounds by moonlight. As a result, flighting becomes irregular. Even so an observant Gun will quickly become aware of any geese which visit his shoot to feed, especially since they are also noisy birds. Once heard, the wild cries of a skein of fighting geese will be indelibly emblazoned on the memory of even the most casual observer.

Spotting activity from duck may well be a lot more difficult, although if you have a large enough area to attract diving ducks such as tufted or pochard, you

Two cock wigeon, young on the left and old on the right, shot over a small splash on a grazing marsh.

will usually see them in daylight. However, the rough shooter rarely has such large waters. His wildfowling ground is more likely to be a small pool, stream or marshy area. In this case, his sport will come from surface-feeding duck like mallard and teal. These birds have a reverse pattern of flighting compared with geese. They normally spend the short winter days resting on some large expanse of water, or other refuge area, and flight to feed under cover of darkness. Flighting takes place in much poorer light than with geese, at the first streak of dawn, and then again in deep dusk. As a consequence, the unobservant sportsman can easily have duck using his shoot without ever noticing the fact. This applies especially since several different species of duck can, at times, come to completely dry areas for food, where the uninitiated might not expect them.

Thus, in September, it may well be that you have a good number of mallard visiting a stubble for spilt grain each evening. Later in the autumn, once the frosts have come, any leftover potatoes can become a magnetic draw. Both a rough ploughed potato stubble or a field which has been subsequently sown to winter corn are likely possibilities, so long as there are some half-rotten, frosted spuds on the surface. Any such areas which also have a few puddles are likely to be even more attractive.

Another common dry ground possibility is offered by wigeon. These birds are basically grazers, and rarely come for grain. Thus, one can find parties coming to pastures or even winter corn fields. However, it must be admitted that they usually like to land on water and walk ashore to graze. A few small splashes only a few feet across may well be all that is needed to attract them if suitable grazing is available nearby.

Under a bright moon, duck flighting patterns can become rather erratic in just the same way as with geese. It is particularly common for duck to arrive late and irregularly at evening time if there is a bright moon up at dusk. Also, if moonrise is expected some while after dark, flighting can often occur a little after moonrise, rather than at the usual time.

Feeding behaviour

Each species of duck and goose has a somewhat distinctive feeding strategy, but there is much overlap between species. However, it is basically true to say that the geese and surface-feeding ducks are mainly vegetarian, while, of the divers, tufted and goldeneye do take animal foods – mainly invertebrates. It is also fair to say that the shoveller is more carnivorous than the other surface feeders, although it may well find that its favoured invertebrates are rather scarce in midwinter.

A reasonable understanding of feeding behaviour will help you to predict which species might visit you, and when. A full-blown account is outside the scope of this book, and anyway, as mentioned earlier, hard and fast rules do not apply. However, there are a few basic truths which may help.

Of the surface-feeding duck, mallard are the most common and perhaps not

Mallard are surface feeders.

surprisingly the most catholic in their tastes. Seeds of one form or another form the bulk of their diet in most circumstances – with those of bur-reed, pond-weed, and other water plants no doubt their main natural diet before man came along with other offerings. Barley and wheat are the two most common food items found in mallard which I have shot over the years, but many other seeds including maize, oats, acorns (from pond or riverside oaks), and various weeds are also seen. Frosted potatoes are a particularly common choice, and I have also found the bulbous roots of various aquatic plants. Various items of animal origin are normal too, and I have often found water snails, freshwater shrimps and even crayfish early in the season. However, such foods are much less frequent in the depths of winter.

Gadwall are, in most respects, a slightly smaller version of the mallard. On the rare occasions when they have come my way they have always been visiting a fed flight pond for corn, and I get the feeling that they are rather less catholic in their tastes than mallard, confining their attentions mainly to the seeds in an aquatic environment.

Pintail rather rarely fall to the lot of the inland shooter. Apart from one or two notable exceptions on floodwaters such as the Ouse Washes, they seem to be mainly coastal in distribution. They are also much inclined to take animal foods, particularly snails, when on the coast. Otherwise various seeds form the bulk of their diet. I have never known them come to a fed flight pond.

Teal are our smallest duck, and again mainly seed eaters in winter. I have rarely known them come to dry stubble fields for spilt corn or rotten potatoes

Pintail are rare inland, but do visit large floods.

in the same way as mallard, but they do take corn if it is available in shallow water, and will often come to feed at flight ponds. However, they do seem to resent the presence of too many mallard in their feeding areas. This often leads them to choose small areas of floodwater, marsh drains and woodland pools which are too small or too enclosed to be really attractive to mallard. Many authors have suggested that teal will graze too, but I have never seen them do it, nor have I found appreciable amounts of grass in any of the several hundred birds which I have dressed for the oven over the years.

Wigeon, however, are grazers first and foremost. Traditionally they were the punt-gunners' duck of the coast, where they fed mainly on beds of eel-grass growing at around low tide mark. They will also graze saltings, inland marshes, pastures and almost any other suitable areas. They do, however, have distinct preferences as to grass species. Turf with a predominance of creeping bent and red fescue seems a particular favourite when inland. There is also no doubt that wigeon like their grass wet wherever possible. They seem to like to land on the water and graze in the shallows, or at any rate to be able to walk gently ashore to graze.

The rather comical looking shoveller has a huge bill.

It would be quite wrong to suggest that wigeon never take seeds, but I have never known them to come enthusiastically to such resources. I believe that on the odd occasions when they come to a fed splash or pool they are really coming because there is suitable grazing anyway. In such circumstances they will take the corn on offer too, but even so I have never shot a wigeon with a bulging crop of corn.

The shoveller is rather an odd-ball amongst the surface feeders, with its huge bill specially adapted to filter feeding for small invertebrates in shallow water. However, in winter such resources can be scarce in the cold waters. In these circumstances, shoveller seem to increase the proportion of seeds and other vegetable matter in their diet.

The diving ducks have a completely different feeding strategy, as their name implies. Diving involves greater energy exertion than dabbing, so these species tend to take larger food items to justify the effort involved.

Goldeneye are said to be largely carnivorous and I must confess that I rarely bother to shoot them. However, the few that I have shot have made perfectly good eating. All contained aquatic invertebrates like shore crabs and winkles, and I assume that equivalent freshwater items are taken inland.

Tufted duck are also quite inclined to take invertebrates such as freshwater shrimps, pea mussels and so on. However, they will also take the roots and tubers of various aquatic plants.

Pochard are said to be the most vegetarian of the diving ducks, and the stonewort is considered to be a staple food. Other aquatic plants are taken too. My friend Nick Giles and his colleagues of The Game Conservancy Trust and ARC Wetland Centre made a study of winter pochard diet on one group of gravel pits near Milton Keynes. Distribution over the pits was found to be far from random. The pochard used areas where the lake bed contained high populations of midge larvae (bloodworms) and these proved to be the major item in the crops of shot birds.

Pochard dive for their food.

Canada geese are largely grazers.

All four of our quarry geese are basically grazing birds in winter. However, there are some distinct differences between the species. The whitefronted seems to stick fairly rigidly to grazing as its feeding strategy, with natural permanent pastures as its favourite choice. Unlike the Canada goose, it rarely even turns to winter cereal fields as a food source. Even the Canada largely retains its grazing strategy when other food offers itself. This is all the more strange when one realises that the migratory Canada goose of North America seems to turn to such foods as spilt maize on a regular basis.

Use of man's farming leftovers is also mirrored by our own wintering pinkfoot and greylag geese. Both these species seem to take stubble gleanings on arrival in the early autumn, moving on to frosted potatoes when the stubbles are either picked bare or ploughed up. Later still they will often return to stubbles, now greened over, to graze the growing cereal plants. At the same time they will move to growing winter cereals and pastures. In certain areas, pinkfeet in particular seem quite fond of carrots, but I get the feeling that this is not really a favourite food, but rather one which will do when other resources fail.

Alongside these basic food preferences, wildfowl also seem to have traditional favourite feeding areas. This applies particularly to geese, which often come to a given area in winter year after year, ignoring other apparently suitable areas for no known reason. Two examples illustrate this well. One is in relation to pinkfeet in Lancashire, which have particular 'goose fields', which are favoured as feeding grounds to the extent that some farmers will avoid growing particularly vulnerable crops on these fields, knowing that they will otherwise get unacceptable trouble. The second is an area of playing fields in South Wales, which used to be a favourite small goose marsh for whitefronts. Normally geese are never seen there now, but just occasionally, in hard weather, a gaggle of whitefronts are seen using this traditional wintering ground on their journey westwards to avoid the worst of the frost.

Morning flight

On a normal winter dawn, wildfowl will be on the move in two basic directions. Duck which have been feeding under cover of darkness will be heading for their daytime refuges, while geese will be heading off to their feeding grounds after a long night of fasting on their safe roost. This gives the wildfowler enormous scope for a shot or two, and perhaps to achieve a mixed bag, if he has both duck and geese in his area.

The first moves will be made by duck, and I hesitate to guess how many dawns I have spent listening to wigeon passing overhead so early that I have been unable to see them in the near total darkness. More often than not, the first thing that you see is not a wigeon at all, but an early teal that skims over so low as to almost take your hat off. As the light grows, one begins to glimpse more duck, with wigeon and mallard being the early movers, and, on average, teal a little later. If there are pintail around, they often seem to come in slightly better light.

The duck flight is usually over before the geese begin to move, although an odd early single pinkfoot can appear in the very first light. Pinks seem to move before greys, and it has often been after sunrise when the first greylags have shown when I have been lucky enough to be awaiting flight in an area where both species are present. Canadas seem to me to be less regular about their flight time, but on some occasions at least they have been distinctly late – to the extent that you could easily be on your way to breakfast when they start to move.

With such a wide range of possible widlfowling sport at dawn, not to mention the chance of a flighting snipe too, it is wise to have a basic plan in mind. Taking your chance on what will arrive can easily result in you not getting a shot at either duck or geese. You will usually be better off to have a particular quarry in mind and then take other offers when they arise.

Morning flight in the fields for geese gives a good example. The geese at roost are probably several miles away, so there is no risk of disturbance by a shot at duck. Indeed, provided that the rough shooter has permission to shoot duck and geese, he is probably wise to load up with small shot for duck, even if geese are the prime aim. Geese rarely arrive without calling, so there should be plenty of time to change over to goose cartridges even if there is not a lull between duck and goose flighting. Such mixed sport is comparatively infrequent. In most cases the waiting Gun expects either duck or geese, and he should set himself up accordingly.

Most successful dawn duck flights are had at daytime resting places – big rivers, lakes, gravel pits and so on. The trick is to know where the birds will come and be in place accordingly. Even so, they can often come in over quite a wide area. At first light there is not much that you can do about this, but the flight often lasts into quite reasonable light conditions, in which case a well placed pattern of decoys can work wonders in pulling the late comers into shot. (The principles of using decoys are discussed in greater detail in Chapter 14.)

You can at times intercept duck which are flighting over your ground to a daytime resting place some distance away. The trick here is to work out the exact flightline which the birds use, and to be on it. The most likely places are along river valleys, but I do know of flightlines over other country. Unless it's early season, however, the duck will rarely flight low enough to be in shot. You will need a really stormy morning to force them to fly low in an attempt to avoid the brunt of the blow.

Wherever possible, it always pays to choose a wild morning for dawn flight. It seems that being shot at in rough conditions disturbs duck less, and the fact that the strong wind forces them to fly lower is also a help. The importance of the disturbance factor cannot be stressed too highly. Birds moving at dawn are in search of peace and security. If you shoot too often or too long you will drive the birds away in search of pastures new. Always be prepared to take it easy, and try to leave the birds in peace before the flight is fully over.

Morning flights at geese are a rather different affair. The shoreline fowler will be trying to intercept birds on route to their feeding grounds, but most shots at geese are probably fired at birds arriving on their inland feeding grounds. Here again, decoys are the key to success, especially since geese usually arrive in fairly good light. They are extremely wary birds, usually less than inclined to fly within shot of any sort of cover which might conceal a hidden gunner. Early in the season it may be easy to tempt them in shot of your hiding place in hedge, ditch or wall, but by late autumn they will usually be giving such cover a fairly wide berth. Success relies on a combination of three factors: a well-organised decoy pattern, good calling, and total concealment.

A careful reconnaissance on a previous morning will often give you useful clues as to where you should be. It may well be that there are favoured parts of a large field, and these can be used to your advantage.

When geese arrive over their chosen field, they may just pile in to feed, provided that they have hardly ever been shot at. Much more normal behaviour, once the season is under way, is for the skein to circle once or twice to ascertain that all is well, and then to drop carefully in. This final approach is invariably into the wind.

In my rather limited experience I have found that it is virtually impossible to pull geese to the upwind end of a field unless this is their favoured area anyway. However, they will often be prepared to drop a little short of their chosen destination in the middle of the field. My most successful flights have involved hiding at the downwind end of the field and setting my decoys behind me. In this way birds have been persuaded to drop low enough to come within range of the downwind edge of the field.

Good cover is essential, and the Gun who finds that nature has not provided enough should take steps to improve the position. The other vital consideration is patience. If the geese are circling overhead, out of range, keep still and keep your face hidden. If you do so, the chances are that they will circle round and come lower next time. Sneak a glance over your shoulder to see if they are coming and you will blow your chance.

In certain rare circumstances, geese will come all day to a chosen field – especially if they are being disturbed from other nearby feeding grounds. This gives a golden opportunity to be greedy. Do not take it. If you leave early and allow the latecomers to come in, you may well find that you can have another go in a week or two over the same field. Geese are the most fantastic birds, and many fowlers have sickened of shooting them after over-indulgence, or given up simply because they find them too wonderful to shoot any more. They deserve better than over-exploitation by greedy people, so set yourself a personal limit and when you reach it stop. Many fowlers would also question the morality of shooting geese over decoys after morning flight proper is over. By an hour after sunrise you will either have made a bag, missed your birds, or come to the conclusion that your homework was insufficient and that you are in the wrong place. In all such cases, it is really time to go home to breakfast, and leave the birds in peace.

Evening flight

At around sunset, the geese will be off to their roost and the coastal fowlers will no doubt be hoping for a skein to come low enough to offer a shot. Inland shooters rarely get much evening sport. Occasionally you might hit off a flightline along which the skeins pass in shot on a stormy night, but such situations are rare, and the geese always seem to fly higher at evening time anyway. For the inland shooter, evening flight is mostly about duck.

I suppose that more wild duck are shot over inland flight pools at dusk than in any other circumstance. Indeed it may even be that the total shot in this way exceeds all the rest put together. The most common quarry at such places is undoubtedly the mallard, but lucky people will have their share of teal too.

Most duck will arrive at deep dusk, so cover is not so important as for geese. However, a good screen is a great help for any early arrivals, and when more than one Gun is shooting the same pool, hides are a valuable safety factor; so long as everyone stays put there is no risk of someone not knowing where his companions are in the dark.

Some Guns who have no trouble estimating range in daylight seem very prone to shooting at birds before they are really in range come flight time. This is a great pity, since it spoils the sport for all, and also risks wounding. A duck which has started circling around a pool at dusk has, in effect, announced its intention to come in, so a little patience should result in a better offer. Having said this, it is also silly to wait too long. Once there is a fair offer, it is best to take it. Duck which are allowed to drop below the skyline are impossible to see clearly – and, if you are in company, shots at such birds are likely to be dangerous anyway. Also, there may be other duck following but some distance off. Wait too long before you shoot at the first group and you may well scare potential subsequent offers.

If you are very lucky a good number of duck may well come to your pond for natural food. This applies particularly in good acorn years, if these wash or drop into your pool from nearby oaks. In most cases, however, the key to regular success with a flight pool is to feed it. Mallard and teal will both take barley if it is offered, and barley tailings or lights are usually easy to obtain from friendly farmers provided that you ask early. The trick is to ask well before harvest, and arrange to store them yourself. The offer of a brace of birds, a flight at duck, or perhaps a bottle of malt is likely to secure what you need, since tailings have virtually no commercial value except for feeding flight ponds. Broken-down chest freezers make remarkably good vermin-proof stores for grub of this kind, and can be sited either at home or by your pond. In the latter case, do take the trouble to paint them green or brown and hide them in the bushes so that they are not a blot on the landscape.

The way to feed a duck pond is to scatter your tailings daily in the shallows just before flight time. The earlier you feed, the more of your grub is taken by moorhens, rats and other scavengers. If you cannot make daily visits, do not imagine that dumping a load of food in the water once a week will do instead. Duck which do not receive a regular ration will soon decide to make use of someone else's hospitality. Daily feeding of just the right amount is essential to real success.

Automatic feeders are a good alternative for those who cannot visit daily. Most are expensive, at £300 to £400, but a motor-spinner and timer kit is available for around a third of this figure. DIY experts will have no trouble fitting this to a suitable waterproof drum with legs to support it.

The correct way to feed a pool, by scattering food in the shallows just before flight time. *(Ian McCall, The Game Conservancy Trust)*

Feeding should start at around the end of July, so as to establish the habit of visiting you in the minds of the home-bred duck. If you do not start early, there is a serious risk that you will not see any duck until Christmas. If you find lots of food still present when you go round next morning, reduce the rate of feeding until all the grub is cleared up each night. Then you can gradually begin to increase the daily ration in the hope that your visitors are recruiting some friends to join the feast. Under-feeding obviously reduces your potential sport, but over-feeding does too. Birds which are offered more than plenty will often feed again at dawn and be late to leave in the morning. As a result they may not be very hungry at dusk, and can decide to wait until well after dark before flighting.

Once you have a good number coming in it is time to arrange a flight. Try not to choose a clear, quiet, starry night. Your birds are much more likely to come in ones and twos in a strong wind, and the sound of your shooting is blown away by the noise of the wind, so there is less disturbance. Once you have had a shot or two, be prepared to leave before the flight is over, so that a lead-in is left for next time. In the long run you will get more sport by doing so. Alan Savory's words at the beginning of this chapter say it all.

Do, however, try to retrieve all shot birds before you leave. Wounded duck should never be left to suffer overnight without the most scrupulous search. Flight pool shooting has a high risk of lost birds, if only because of the poor light. It really should not be contemplated without the help of dogs. Some shooters prefer to leave the picking-up until the end, but I would rather get on with it as the birds fall. I have known too many 'dead' duck which have turned into runners to trust to my luck in this regard. Also, if you pick up as you go along, you can get away quicker once you have decided to stop, thus leaving the lead-in in peace.

Daytime flight

Under certain circumstances you can enjoy superb flights at duck in broad daylight. On really rough days duck often seemed inclined to move about almost for the joy of flying in a big wind. If you are lucky enough to have a shoot which includes a piece of river valley or a big lake of some sort, some good sport is a possibility. The trick is to try to find a sheltered patch of water, anchor a few decoys, hide yourself well, and await events.

Once the gale has been raging for hours, most birds will have found shelter and they will stick to it, but if you hit off a rising wind, your chances are good. It seems that, as their life becomes too uncomfortable, and particularly if the waves get really big, the birds move for calmer waters. Most often this is a sheltered bend of the river, or a quiet corner of the lake, but a nearby small water can be chosen too. I well remember one such flight to a small patch of floodwater about half a mile from a large area of open water.

Those shooters who have a relatively sheltered patch of water close to the coast may enjoy good daylight flights too, due to the effect of the tide. Duck which are resting in an estuary are often prone to flight as the tide rises. This is especially so in rough weather, as the waves on the estuary can get really big – even when the wind is only a Force 6 or 7, rather than a full gale.

Moonflighting

As mentioned earlier in this chapter, both ducks and geese can move under the moon. This can present some of the most exciting shooting ever, but it is far from easy to predict. Also, just because there is a moon up do not expect to see your quarry. A clear bright moonlight night is a wildfowler's nightmare. Everything is bathed in an unearthly glow, but you cannot actually see the birds in flight. What you need is a pale sky of fleecy cloud against which your birds are visible and identifiable in silhouette. Given such ideal conditions it is possible to see a teal at up to about 100 yards, and geese to at least twice that range, so do not be tempted to shoot too soon. Wait until they are really in range.

Movement of geese under the moon seems to be more predictable than duck. Geese will often flight soon after moonrise, and your chances of a shot if you hide beside a favourite feeding field are good. Also, because the light is poorer than normal morning flight conditions, you do not need such an elaborate hide. In my experience you will rarely get it right, but if you do, the birds can come very well so, again, there is the risk of overdoing the bag. If you are really lucky, do not forget the self-imposed limit mentioned earlier. Once you have enough for your own consumption, and perhaps one or two to give away to deserving friends, stop and leave the geese in peace.

Soon after moonrise seems to be a good bet with duck too, although in my experience they are less reliable than geese. I have a strong feeling that on a moonlight night they move all night long, and there is often little enough pattern to the movement. If you are close to a coastal resting site, a flooding tide can have a similar effect to that noted under daylight flighting. Birds will often go much further at night though, turning up at feeding grounds many miles inland. If evening flight fails, waiting for moonrise or high tide can both be distinct possibilities.

Walking-up

If you are fortunate enough to have a piece of ground with ditches, streams or other watercourses, it can pay off to walk these at the start of your day. A few duck will often hang around such places all day long, but if you start shooting elsewhere they will probably be off to find a quieter corner. Walking straight along such ditches will be largely a waste of time. Most of the birds will see you coming and be off before you are in shot. To be successful you need to creep up at right angles and look into the ditch or stream. Long straight stretches are always a problem. If there are plenty of birds you will probably get a shot, but usually there are only one or two. However, given time you will learn which are the favourite spots, and thus where you are likeliest to get a shot. Take full advantage of any bends, and any bankside bushes to break your network into separate stretches which can be stalked individually. Also, use the wind to your advantage. Stalking into the wind is helpful in masking the sound of your approach, and in giving you a straight away shot at your bird as it rises into the wind. Also, if you work your ground as a whole into the wind, the sound of your shooting will carry less far over the unshot areas which hopefully harbour further birds.

Walking-up like this can be very disruptive if there are large numbers of birds present. In these circumstances you should think hard about the question of flighting. An area which holds appreciable numbers of birds during the day might well be more productively shot as a morning flight.

Driving

Driving hand-reared duck falls outside the scope of this book, but there are truly wild birds which can be driven. When working ditches in the manner described above, it can pay off to hide another Gun or two on the expected exit route of any birds which might flush.

Diving ducks, in particular, can be amenable to driving operations. A good example which I know well is given by two gravel pits which are about 200 yards apart. If the birds on either pit are disturbed, they head for the other. The recipe here is for the majority of the Guns to hide half-way between the two pits. One member of the party then goes to the far end of pit one and fires a shot. This shifts the birds which flight over the hidden Guns. Quite often, the sound of their shooting is enough to flush the birds on pit two, which proceed to head for pit one and offer a return drive. Otherwise, once the first flight is over, someone goes to the end of pit two and flushes the birds as before.

This shooting over dry land has another advantage. The shot birds will fall before they reach the water and any wounded birds will be easy to gather.

Diving duck such as tufted are usually easier to drive than surface feeders.

Wing-tipped diving duck are the very devil to retrieve since they dive so much more strongly than surface feeders.

Extremely exciting drives can be had at geese too. The trick, again, is to conceal the Guns on the expected exit route of the birds and then flush them. Geese will usually have distinct ideas about where they want to go when flushed. They will take off into the wind and then move off in their chosen direction. However, they will usually start by heading away from the direction of the approaching danger which flushed them. Also if there are any number, they will form into a skein quite quickly, and a skein of 200 geese forms a line well over 200 yards long. So, exactly where the Guns go is not *that* critical. The most important factor is that they must get into a good, well-hidden position without being seen. This is the difficult bit. Show your backside above the cover as you crawl into your chosen position, and if you are within 200 or 300 yards the quarry will be away.

The closer you can get, the better your chances. It is sensible to synchronise watches with the Gun doing the driving because if he can see you getting into position it is a fair bet that the geese can too.

Many shooters would consider goose driving in this fashion unsporting. However, it does require considerable skill to get into position undetected, and even then the odds are on the geese. In my experience no more than one in three drives is successful, and you cannot fit many into a short winter's day. As with all such things, sportsmanship has a lot to do with respect for the quarry. If you are careful not to be greedy, a drive or two does little harm and it can be very exciting. In my experience the disturbance to the birds is minimal; nine times out of ten they are back in position later on the same day and they are virtually always back by the following day. Morning flight, on the other hand, can put them off completely if overdone.

The question of sportsmanship in relation to geese has been mentioned several times in this chapter, but duck have had less of a mention in this respect. All sportsmen will be quick to remember that the majority of our wildfowl are migrants which only come in winter. We are the guardians of a wonderful sporting resource which we share with many other nations. Short-term greed in the United Kingdom would inevitably lead to long-term declines, *and* get us a bad name with overseas sportsmen. If you are lucky enough to enjoy some sport with duck or geese, treat them with the respect which they are due. Do not take long shots and do not overshoot. You will enjoy your sport more for knowing that you are being fair and reasonable.

As a last point please remember that there are very few circumstances where you could legally shoot wildfowl with lead anywhere in Britain. This is explained in more detail on page 58. Please also remember that the Code of Good Shooting Practice calls on all of us to avoid use of lead shot over wetlands of significance to feeding waterfowl.

13

Pigeons

'That naughty bird *Columba palumbus*, the ring-necked dove or wood pigeon, is indeed a bad boy and does a vast amount of harm to all members of the farming fraternity. He will also eat all the green stuff in your back garden as a side line. Nevertheless, I am very fond of him, though I do make my living out of his destruction.'

Archie Coats *Pigeon shooting* (1963)

Natural history

The wood pigeon shares a problem with rabbits and hares. It is potentially a serious agricultural pest. However, the tenant farmer does not have an inalienable right, as he does with rabbits and hares, to control the pigeon. This means that the rough shooter needs to exercise great care over his shooting leases. If he retains the right to pigeon control, he must expect to do the job to the farmer's satisfaction or face the consequences – and perhaps the compensation claims.

The alternative is to make sure of a lease in which the farmer retains the right and responsibility to control pigeons. In practice this is probably the better plan, especially if you make a point of getting on well with your farmer. Given a reasonable approach on both sides, he will probably ask you to do something about the pigeons if they are a problem, before setting about the job himself.

There are a number of species of wild pigeons in the United Kingdom, of which only the wood pigeon and the collared dove can be shot legally. Feral domestic pigeons are quite common around many towns, and even along coasts in their natural 'rockdove' habitat. These feral pigeons may be shot, but both the ancestral stock of truly wild rockdoves of the north-western coasts, and the racing or homing pigeon are protected, the latter by virtue of being the valued property of their owners. All these three birds are of the same species and thus easily confused. You should never take a shot at a passing feral pigeon – it is quite likely to be a racer. Only consider shooting feral pigeons as they come into a crop where you know that they are causing damage.

The greatest risk of a mistake for the pigeon shooter is the stock dove. This is a common bird in much of the British Isles, and is quite similar to the wood pigeon. It is slightly smaller but, as any bird-watcher will tell you, size alone is difficult to judge if you do not have the two birds side-by-side. The flight pattern is very similar to a wood pigeon too, although wing beats are a little quicker on average. Two factors to look out for are a comparatively shorter and more tapered tail, and the colour pattern of the underwing. This is pale in the centre with dark leading and trailing edges, and is quite obvious in good light. The fact that the stock dove does not have the white wing flashes of the wood pigeon is less helpful than you expect, as you often fail to notice this on a pigeon anyway, especially if it is coming in high.

The collared dove is very different from the wood pigeon, being much smaller and paler. Its plumage has a pinkish tinge, and its flight is much more jerky. It is also very much a bird of farmyards, hen runs, gardens and parks, where it feeds on spilt grain. Damage to field crops is minimal, but grain spoilage in granaries can be quite high. Again, there is potential for confused identification, in this case with the protected turtle dove. This bird is a summer visitor to southern Britain, where it also often frequents farmyards. The key identification feature is that the turtle dove has a rich chestnut-brown back with darker centres to the feathers giving a scaly appearance. It also has a different pattern of colours and marks on the tail. The turtle dove's tail is darker above, but both have white edging. Both species have a dark underside to the tail with white tip, but that on the turtle dove is much narrower. The collared dove is not often a rough-shooter's quarry. However, standing a few Guns in a farmyard where there are too many collared doves can provide a fast and furious ten minutes of sport before they all depart for quieter quarters. If you are then prepared to wait, you may well be rewarded with a steady trickle of returning birds for an hour or more. If you do make a bag of collared doves in this way, do not waste them as ferret food. They are delicious eating and well worth the trouble to pluck and dress. Unlike wood pigeons, they never resort to grazing such third-rate foods as rape or kale, but stick entirely to seeds. As a result they are always in good condition, and never take on the rank flavour exhibited by the odd pigeon which has been feeding on frosted brassica crops.

Both pigeons and collared doves are tree nesters, although odd birds will choose the most surprising sites. Pigeons, for example have been known to nest on the ground in heather moorland areas where there are no trees. Both species have a normal clutch of just two white eggs, and the young are fed on 'pigeons' milk'. This is produced from the thickened lining of the crop of both parents and thence regurgitated to the young. Breeding can occur at any time of year, and is mainly governed by food availability and the physical condition of the adults. As a result, most wood pigeons breed in late summer and autumn, when the abundant food of ripening cereals makes living easy.

Food choice and crop damage

The wood pigeon is mainly a seed-eating bird. However, if seeds are in short supply it will take the buds and shoots of an enormous range of plants. The problem for the pigeon is that its digestive system is not frightfully good at using these poorer grade foods and as a consequence it needs to spend almost all its waking hours feeding to obtain enough nutrition.

The pigeon is also a very gregarious bird. Once one finds a good food source, others will join in until a huge flock forms, if the size of the resource allows. This is where the pigeon comes into conflict with the farmer. Not only does it feed on his crops, but it chooses to do so *en masse*. The degree of damage can be far greater than the uninitiated might expect. A good example is the destruction of a field of mature cabbages. Pigeons will move slowly along taking two or three pecks from the heart of each cabbage, thereby ruining the entire plant. Just to add insult to injury, they will defecate on others, and this is the sort of garnish which the housewife is apt to complain about when she gets her cabbage from the greengrocer!

Pigeons are remarkably good at finding the best feeding which is available locally. As a consequence rigid tables of feeding month by month are apt to break down. If you want to know what the local pigeons are doing for a living, there is only one reliable way to find out – go and look. Archie Coats said it all: 'Time spent in reconnaissance is seldom wasted.' My friend John Batley, who has followed in Archie's footsteps as a professional, normally spends only three days each week shooting, using the other four to study the form. Amateurs will need even more study if they are to expect any good days.

The master at work: Archie Coats (right) and a friend setting out decoys. *(The Game Conservancy Trust)*

An approximate timetable can be created. I stress again what was said above – it is far from infallible. Exceptions keep proving the rule. However, according to the time of year, you should be searching out your birds in crops and growth described below.

As soon as spring drilling starts you can expect flocks on the newly drilled fields looking for spilt grains. This applies to corn, peas, beans and other more specialist crops. Meantime the birds will also be grazing the new spring growth. Oilseed rape and clover are two of the most likely choices, but I have found them hard at work on dandelions in pasture and chickweed in horticultural areas.

As summer comes along they will often switch to newly emerging peas for a few days, but once the corn begins to swell this is a favourite choice. Patches of laid corn caused by summer storms are a particular favourite. Once the first crops are harvested, they usually move to stubbles for spilt grain. This again need not be just cereals, for peas, beans and rape are all taken. This is the time of plenty for pigeons and also the peak breeding season.

The ripening of autumn nuts heralds a change and these become a favourite food. Acorns and beech mast are two special choices, and they are probably nearer the natural food of pigeons in times past. It is clear that even two centuries ago the pigeon was far from the common agricultural pest which it is today. Indeed, Gilbert White in his classic *The Natural History and Antiquities of Selborne* (1789) notes that autumn pigeons feeding on the acorns and mast in the woods were a much prized sporting attraction.

As the days shorten to midwinter the pigeons continue with their stubble gleanings and nuts for as long as possible. They will also often choose to graze post-harvest weeds as the supply of seeds runs low. In one area of the Hampshire/Dorset border which I shoot regularly in December and January, pigeons with a mixed crop of grain, and chickweed shoots are quite common.

This is the time of year when the modern pigeon shooter expects them to begin to hammer the winter oilseed rape. It is my impression, however, that rape is very much a last resort when other foods run out. There is also no doubt that pigeons which are forced to live entirely on rape during these shortest midwinter days lose condition rapidly. As far as I can see, there are not enough daylight hours in late December for a pigeon to eat sufficient rape, or indeed kale or other brassicas, for it to survive in the long term. By the end of January, however, it is a different story. So long as snow does not cover the food so thickly that the pigeon cannot get to it, the worst is over. A late January day is about two hours longer than the shortest day, and a pigeon can pack a lot of rape into its crop in the extra two hours.

Even now, however, rape is not really a favourite choice. As soon as other foods present themselves the pigeons switch. A surprising number of pigeons shot coming to roost on February evenings will contain other foods, even in rape growing areas. One good example is ivy berries. Once these begin to ripen, every hedgerow ivy will have its complement of a dozen pigeons eagerly gathering up the spoils. My old friend Eric Roderick knows all about this, and shoots more pigeons in February and March by sitting under ivy clad trees in his West Wales hedges than at any other time of the year, unless he is lucky enough to get a good session on a barley stubble.

Apart from midwinter, when they are forced to feed virtually all day long, pigeons have a distinct daily routine. This is to some extent dictated by their 'digestive bottleneck', the term used to describe the fact that they can eat faster than they can digest. As a consequence, even in the depths of winter, pigeons do not feed really hard all day long. However, given the need to conserve energy, they will often remain in their chosen field throughout the day, feeding steadily but not avidly until an hour or so before sunset when the rate of pecking goes up, so that they can go to roost on a full crop.

During the longer days of spring, summer and autumn, pigeons will usually come off the roost soon after it gets light, and go to feed for an hour or two until mid-morning. They then fly off to 'sitty' trees in hedgerows and woodland edges where they loaf around until midday, when another rather half-hearted feed is in order. By early to mid-afternoon, according to day length, it is time to feed in earnest. It is thus fair to say that one of the best times to shoot over decoys is from lunchtime onwards. Very early starts *can* be productive too, and I well remember one late August morning in Wales when a stiff blow provided some really testing sport between 6 o'clock and breakfast time. However, afternoon is almost always more reliable given the right weather conditions.

John Batley pointed out to me recently, that pigeons have distinct tastes, too, in terms of 'sitty' trees. Given the choice, they will usually loaf around in ash trees, whether these be hedgerow standards or the ones along woodland edges where they choose to rest during the day. A moment of reflection shows that these trees often combine a little extra height with a fairly open canopy. This no doubt provides a good lookout post and ease of access without wearing out the flight feathers.

Shooting over decoys

It must be true that the majority of the pigeons which are shot in the United Kingdom are killed in the fields over decoys. This is a sport which has produced many expert proponents over the years, and there is an enormous selection of good books on the subject. It would be quite wrong, therefore, for me to try to cover the subject in a few words in just one chapter. Anyone who is serious about his pigeon shooting should certainly consult the words of the late Archie Coats. His *Pigeon Shooting* was first published in 1963, and a new edition came out in 1990, having been brought up to date just before he died. Unlike so many second and third editions, Archie never felt the need to rip up the first try and rewrite. He knew what he was writing about in 1963, and did not see the need to do more than update a few points. This surely is the mark of a master craftsman and a good book. 'The Basics are still the same.'

Most of my own ideas about pigeon decoying, decoy choice and decoy

Your decoys must show well. *(The Game Conservancy Trust)*

layout are distilled into the next chapter. I will, however, reiterate one or two points, and add a few fine details which I hope might help. First and foremost, and at risk of saying it *ad nauseam*, do your homework. Go out and watch what the birds are at, and get yourself under the traffic. Your decoys must show well, and you must be well hidden in a good hide with a good background.

There is no doubt that windy and dull weather is best. Birds decoy better in these conditions. John Batley is also sure that a falling atmospheric pressure helps. He believes that the birds like to face a period of stormy weather with a full crop. It has certainly been my experience that really wet days are bad news, since pigeons try to find some shelter and stay put until things settle down. Since a falling glass usually coincides with a rising wind and overcast conditions, all things come together to give you a good chance.

The importance of keeping still and hidden as your birds approach cannot be stressed too highly. Pigeons have all-round vision so that they can see flying predators approaching when they are on the feed. As a consequence they can see you clearly enough if you move. In flight, they will soon see your moving pale face down below; it is very obvious, so do not show it – keep still and wait until the pigeon is in range. As a pigeon commits itself to join your decoys it spreads its tail to form an airbrake. At the same moment its all-round eyes both turn forward to give binocular vision of the landing point which avoids a crash. At that moment, the pigeon will be concentrating so hard that it will not see you as you steal your gun into your shoulder and shoot. If you miss, the pigeon will be off like a rocket, so do let it get well in range for the first shot or you will be tempted to take an unfairly long shot at a departing bird. Pigeons may be an agricultural pest, but they deserve the same respect as any other quarry in terms of excessive range shooting. Long shots are also a waste of cartridges.

Summer along the hedgerows

In the height of summer, pigeons do not seem to flock up to the same extent as at other times of year. A combination of localised food resources in the form of small laid patches, and the opportunity to spend much of the day sitting around digesting food means that they are scattered all over the countryside. At this time of year decoying can be unrewarding, and shooting over laid patches poses problems in relation to setting of decoys and gathering of the slain anyway. You will be very unpopular with the farmer if you tread down either the standing crop or the laid patch, which may well be only half down anyway. Also, if you sit around for long, flies can get distinctly bothersome as well. Insect repellents are a help, but they just stop them from settling and you still finish up with a buzzing mob around you.

A worthwhile alternative is to walk slowly around your ground along the thicker and taller hedges. Pigeons will often flush in range, dropping down from their perches to gain speed and offering fast testing shots under the spreading branches as they go. In solid arable country you have the same problem over collecting shot birds, but in most areas some of the farming is mixed and you can often choose to shoot alongside mown grass, farm tracks or in other situations where there is not a standing crop. If you have to shoot in corn, a dog is much less heavy than you, and rarely pushes down an appreciable amount of crop in fetching birds, provided that it is not the sort which is forever jumping over the corn to locate its position.

This is obviously a sport of warm weather, and you will therefore be lightly clad. Chances are, that even if you don a jacket it will soon be committed to your bag as you warm up. Do not forget to choose a sensibly coloured shirt. If you do, and you freeze when you first spot them, you will often get fair offers at flighting birds too.

Winter evenings and roost shooting

As well as feeding communally in the fields, pigeons normally roost together in the woods. This applies particularly in winter, when huge numbers can come in together to chosen areas. Such assemblages provide tremendous sport as the birds come twisting through the treetops on their final approach.

The best possible options are comparatively small woods in largely arable areas, where the birds are effectively faced with 'Hobson's Choice' in their selection of roost sites. However, good roosting places are rarely at such a premium, and the wise roost shooter will study his ground and his birds carefully, in choosing where to go.

In wild weather particularly, pigeons tend to favour conifers for the extra shelter which they afford. A clump of pine, larch, western hemlock or similar in an otherwise deciduous wood is a good choice. Indeed, such trees standing a little above the rest seem to act as a beacon to the birds. If you can watch from a vantage point outside such a wood you will see the birds trickling into the conifer areas a few at a time from about an hour before sunset.

If there are no conifers, the ash trees already mentioned are another favoured choice, although beech and oak are often used too. As a general principle it seems that the larger trees are chosen, and I suspect that this is because they sway around rather less in the wind. I have a strong suspicion too that the birds like to settle in a good vantage point to start with, and then drop down a little lower to a warmer spot once they are satisfied that all is safe. One particular favourite spot in a wood of my acquaintance is an area of an acre or so of mature ash which has been underplanted by a mix of western hemlock and Norway spruce. Nearly all the birds first land in the ash trees, but they spend the night down below in the hemlocks.

All this study of which trees are likely only gives you half the answer. The other half is to walk round under the trees during daytime and look for the heaviest concentrations of pigeon droppings. These are white splashes, and not the solid sort of droppings produced by roosting pheasants.

If you are shooting as part of an 'organised' pigeon shoot on a February evening, weather considerations will be ignored. With a Gun or two in every wood, you should be assured of some sport, so long as you do not share your wood with a Gun who is prone to long shots. This can be a miserable business. A flock of birds are wheeling overhead, just out of range and set to come in when some idiot elsewhere in the wood lets drive and ruins everyone's chances. Do not be greedy for shooting, wait until they really are coming in and then choose your birds carefully.

When you are going to shoot alone, or with just a few chosen companions who can come at short notice, try to select a windy evening. Just as with duck flighting, or indeed pigeon decoying, wilder weather means that your shooting is less disruptive to the birds. Flocks are often smaller too, and the birds come in low over the trees rather than circling high, folding their wings, and dropping like stones. All this adds up to better shooting.

You will rarely need to build a hide for such shooting, the main consideration for concealment is to keep still. However, it does pay to choose your clothing with care, and to take up a position with a good background. Standing in front of a thick tree trunk or a large bush is a good idea. Also, remember to keep your face turned down as far as possible when you spot your birds. You should peer at them through your eyebrows. A woolly balaclava helmet, pulled down over your face, is a great help in dry weather, but a real bugbear when it is wet. It can also be very uncomfortable when it is cold and your breath condenses on to the fabric making it soggy. Lastly, if there is a chance of members of the public strolling about your wood, remember that a balaclava can have them thinking of armed terrorists these days. This is especially so if you team it with a camouflage jacket. Police over-reaction to such clothing is not unheard of, and it could waste a lot of your time and spoil your day if you happen to be the victim of a police raid.

If you suffer from the same luck as me when waiting for roosting pigeons, you will for ever find birds dropping in just out of range. This is frustrating in itself, but even more so when further birds keep coming to join those already in. The answer is to try and stalk the bird or birds. You may get a shot, and you will certainly ensure that it does not attract its mates away from you.

Do not be in too much of a rush to start your stalk however. A newly-arrived pigeon spends a minute or so on lookout, with head held high, before its head drops onto its shoulders and the bird settles. Always wait until this has happened before you set off on your stalk. The next thing to do is to choose a tree which you judge to be within range of your bird to use as cover for your approach. You then slip *slowly* sideways until the pigeon is hidden behind this tree and then stalk quietly up, taking care not to crunch any sticks under foot and alarm your bird. Having reached your chosen tree you peer round . . . *et voila*, there is your bird. The choice now is between flushing it for a flying shot, or going for a sitter. Personally, in these circumstances, I am a meat hunter.

Sounds simple does it not? Well it isn't. Usually you find that your tree was not quite close enough, and you are very likely to be rumbled if you move across into view at such close range to try to approach screened by another. In practice I reckon that about one in three stalks result in a shot, and that about half of these are at birds which spot me and flush at the last minute. If you are nearly in range and you see the bird's head pop up, freeze; you have aroused its suspicions, but it might just settle again. Even so, the odds are very much with the pigeon.

Evening roost shooting rarely produces big bags of birds, but it is enormous fun. I do not think I have ever had more than about 20, and 10 is distinctly good. Most evenings seem to produce between 2 and 6, and blanks are not unheard of. You can improve your chances by taking a length of string, a fishing weight, and a solid decoy, and hoisting this into a prominent position at your chosen site. It is, however, far from easy to get such a decoy high enough to really help. Decoys also encourage you to stay in one place and often it is the flexible approach which leads to success. One of the charms of roost shooting is that all you really need is a dog, gun, belt of cartridges and a bag for the spoils if you should be so lucky.

14
Principles of Decoying

'The first bunch passed a quarter of a mile to our left, and I was surprised to see the Old Man begin suddenly kicking his foot up in the air, quickly lowering it, only to kick it up again. In a whisper I asked him why.

"To attract their attention", he answered. "To make them see our stool. From a distance it looks as though a duck in this flock was sitting up and flapping his wings."

Suddenly I saw the passing flock rise fifty feet above the water, and every bird turn towards us as though governed by a single impulse.'

Percy M. Cushing 'The passing of the battery' (1912). In Worth Mathewson *Wildfowling Tales, 1888–1913* (1989)

Of ducktraps and other shams

The word decoy has two very different meanings. Firstly there is the duck trap in the form of a pond with netted 'pipes', believed to be of Dutch origin, which was used to harvest wildfowl before the Gun took command. Then there is the live, stuffed or model animal used to attract live quarry. This latter system for luring birds to their downfall relies on one of two types of behaviour – mobbing or gregariousness.

Songbirds (including the crow family) have a very strong instinct to mob such predators as hawks, owls and even cuckoos. Hence the plastic owl decoys, often with flapping wings which adorn the window displays of many gun shops. This facet of decoying really falls outside the scope of this book except where the rough shooter uses this system as part of his keepering.

On the other hand, several species of prime quarry for the rough shooter are gregarious in behaviour and thus amenable to the use of suitable decoys of their own kind in drawing them into shot. Ducks, geese and pigeons can all be decoyed to representations of their own species, and the principles of using this method apply across the full spectrum.

Rigging a dead pinkfoot in a feeding position. The real thing makes an excellent decoy when well set.

The qualities of a good decoy

A decoy which does not attract its intended victims is obviously useless. As Archie Coats pointed out so many times in relation to pigeons, the real thing is the best decoy of all. Aside from the fact that it is illegal it would also be totally impractical to transport and tether a dozen live pigeons – let alone grey geese. However, dead birds can be set out in lifelike positions to great effect. Indeed I gather that Archie hardly ever used any other form of pigeon decoy.

However, using dead birds does rely on having a ready supply of corpses, no problem to the professional who uses a few of yesterday's score. For the rest of us it means storing birds in the freezer between sessions. This, the weight of the dead, and their comparative fragility has all led to the use of artificials by most people. Once upon a time these were carved from blocks of wood and carefully hand painted, but today most decoys, whether of pigeons, duck or geese, are made from plastic. The modern plastic pigeon and goose shells, which can be stacked inside each other are superbly easy to carry and simple to set out on dry ground. Similarly the swimming duck type have their own built-in weight and keel, and have only to be anchored in a suitable place.

When selecting which decoys to buy you should take care to choose the best type. For example, ducks at rest have their heads tucked low on their shoulders. Some decoys – particularly the type which is made of rubber rather than plastic have excessively long necks which can easily scare approaching birds into thinking that they are about to fly away.

The real difficulty with artificials, however, is that it is virtually impossible

Dead goose and shell (above) compared, and (below) the same thing with pigeons. Note how both artificials shine in an unnatural fashion along their backs.

to prevent them from shining in bright light. This tendency to shine is most unnatural, and will almost always cause approaching birds to shy away just before they come into range. Using the dullest of matt paints obviously helps, but even this is only partially successful.

For the pigeon shooter the answer is to follow Archie Coats: glue a pair of wings, the tail and a strip of skin and feathers from the back onto your artificials. The inland goose shot could, no doubt, do the same thing – although this is less important since he will usually have finished shooting by breakfast time, before the sun is really bright. However, this is obviously impractical for the wildfowler who wishes to float his decoys on a pool, splash, river or creek. All he can do is to choose the dullest paint possible, and float his decoys carefully so that their backs do not get wet. On a sunny day he can at least console himself by admiring the view, watching other birds, and reflecting that wildfowling conditions are not good anyway.

Decoy patterns

When viewing wildfowl out on the open waters, or pigeons hammering a farmer's rape, it is easy to get the impression that they are 'thicker than jam in a pot' with hardly a square inch between the birds. The truth is that our comparatively low profile gives us a very false impression of a flock of birds. An overhead view would reveal that the birds are much more widely spaced than we realise.

A well spread pattern – always space your decoys.

Decoys should be set out in a similar way. Archie Coats always suggested at least 4 yards between his pigeons, and I would suggest about the same for duck and more for geese. Our quarry may be gregarious, but they still have their particular etiquette over 'personal space'. One only has to watch the endless squabbles amongst a gaggle of feeding geese to see how true this is.

Birds, like aeroplanes, take off and land into the wind. They also tend to face into the wind when on the ground (or water). This is not an absolutely rigid rule, but a general trend. You should therefore set your decoys in the same way – with a majority facing roughly into the wind. Except when floated on very strong currents, duck or goose decoys on water will orientate into the wind anyway. Given the choice it can pay to choose a site where wind and current are in agreement to avoid tangled anchor lines.

Different species of birds have a different etiquette about where they join a feeding or resting flock. Pigeons will often fly over those already feeding in a field and look out for a large enough space into which they can land without offending the sensibilities of those already there. Archie Coats used this habit to his advantage by leaving a gap in his decoy pattern in an appropriate place for a reasonably easy shot. This he called his 'killing ground'.

Surface-feeding duck tend to drop into the downwind end of a group already *in situ*, as do geese, so you should set out your decoys with this in mind. You can, to some extent make a 'killing ground' by setting a main group of decoys with a few leading off a short way downwind. Some birds at least, will tend to follow the line of these stragglers up to the tail of your main pattern.

Diving duck are much more inclined to pass over their fellows to find a place at the head of the raft. A pattern in the form of an arrowhead can be very successful in concentrating them in just the right place. This arrowhead or V pattern has advantages for both behaviour types. Overfliers concentrate over the head, and species which drop short land into the V. So long as you know what your particular quarry does, you can set your pattern accordingly.

Successful siting of decoys

'Time spent in reconnaissance is seldom wasted' is a well-known military maxim. Archie Coats applied this to pigeons and successful wildfowlers apply it to duck and geese. Your best efforts with decoys will largely be ignored unless your quarry has at least an inclination to settle in the area where you place them. Observation of their behaviour is therefore essential to real success. Most pigeon shooters spend at least some of their time on some vantage point studying pigeon movements with binoculars. They will also have a thorough knowledge of the cropping in their area, so as to be able to predict likely feeding behaviour. For the inland goose shooter the same principles apply.

Spotting the movements of duck may well be less easy, especially since most activity occurs at dawn or dusk. However, rafts of duck on a sheltered bay of a lake, or a quiet bend of a river are a good indication of a likely dawn flight station, where decoys can be used to advantage. Feeding grounds are often better located by searching for droppings and preened feathers, but decoys are unlikely to help much at evening flight anyway, since most of the birds will arrive when it is too dark for them to see your decoys. In these circumstances, a well-blown call is more likely to help concentrate birds in the right area.

Having hit off the right basic area in which to set up, the next part of the job is to study carefully the local geography and choose the exact place which will provide the best hide. With careful use of decoys it is perfectly possible to attract birds for some yards from their chosen landing area. Thus, it pays to choose a good hiding place even if it is a *little* way off the main flight of your chosen quarry *provided* that your decoys will still show up well. Your quarry will see you very quickly, particularly if you move, if you are not well hidden.

Having chosen a good hiding place, and perhaps embellished it with extra hide materials, you can then set up your decoys so as to try to provide a 'killing ground' where you find it easy to shoot. An example of my own preference is given in the diagram, but it is perhaps as well to explain it more fully. In common with most right-handed shots, I find a right to left crosser easier to kill than the reverse. The perfect place, if I am facing forwards at 12 o'clock is a bird coming in at about 10 o'clock. I therefore set my decoys at about 9 o'clock (for pigeons, geese and surface-feeding duck – it would be 11 o'clock for diving ducks), assuming that the wind is coming from approximately 6 o'clock. Birds settling

Well placed decoys can pull birds a considerable distance. Faced with a huge flood, this fowler needs decoys to concentrate his birds to an area where he can hide.

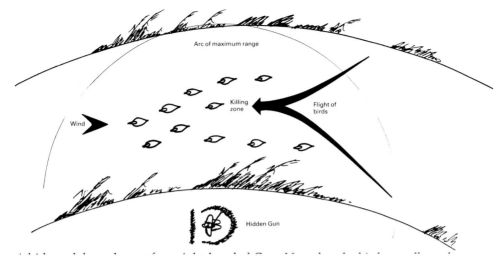

A hide and decoy layout for a right-handed Gun. Note that the birds are allowed to come well in, and that the hide has a good high back. The decoys are drawn large and so appear cramped – they should be well spaced.

into the wind come in from the front and cross to my left. When duck shooting in a strong gale, particularly on a river where wind and flow direction coincide, I would set my decoys further upwind and wait until birds had passed me to between 8 and 9 o'clock, so as to reduce the risk of a wounded bird being whisked away by the combined effects of wind and current. Also, whatever the quarry a second shot is much more likely to score if one lets birds get well in, as they will be getting very rapidly further away from the moment they first spot you. This may be several seconds before you fire even your first shot.

Pulling power

There is nothing so lonely as a single bird, be it duck, goose or pigeon. Singles will therefore come to decoys particularly well. As group size increases, tendency to join with others drops. However, there is another basic rule of thumb: the larger the pattern of decoys, the more attractive it becomes.

In practice, there are limits on how many decoys you will be able to lug around, but half a dozen should usually be considered a bare minimum, with a dozen or more preferable if you can manage it. Bulk and weight are both considerations, and the advent of shell decoys for pigeons and geese is a tremendous boon. Even with a dozen decoys out you will rarely have much effect on large groups of 20 birds or more unless they intend to come to your chosen site anyway. However, singletons will almost invariably be looking for any kind of company, and groups of up to half a dozen or so will often come well too. The flock instinct is stronger in geese than in either duck or pigeon, so large groups of the latter two may be rather loosely associated, and sometimes one or two individuals will peel off from a group to join your decoys. By the same token, because their flock instinct is strong, a big skein of geese may decide to join a small gaggle *if* they are convincingly sited in the right place.

Decoy size is also a consideration and there is no doubt that if transport is not a problem over-sized decoys are more effective – hence the 'magnum' mallard which is so popular in America. However, numbers are also important, as discussed above, and my own feeling is that I would rather have a dozen normal sized decoys than six big ones.

Eye catchers

Quite often when decoying you will see a bird or birds pass by a little way off, whereupon they spot some real birds whom they then join. You get the feeling that they have failed to notice your own setup, and that if they had, they would have joined yours. When this happens with monotonous regularity there is only one conclusion. You are in the wrong spot and it is time to move.

Occasionally, of course, you cannot move, either because there is no cover near where the birds are moving to, or perhaps because you are already at the boundary of your own ground. On other occasions, the quarry traffic is over a broad front so that some do come well – it is just that you would like to attract more. In these circumstances something extra to catch the eye is what is needed.

This can be provided in one of two ways, either by using a few decoys which contrast more strongly with their background, or by adding movement. An example of the first case is the use of a white gull decoy near a pattern of swimming ducks – a technique which was recommended by Stanley Duncan over 80 years ago in *The Complete Wildfowler*. The well-known pigeon flapper system is a good example of the second, and one which undoubtedly works. It is rather an aggravation to carry around and set up a cradle with its dead bird, but if you follow the advice of the professionals and use dead birds as decoys anyway, it is not that much trouble. The trick is to show a distant bird just a couple of flaps of the decoy to simulate a bird settling with others. Archie Coats simply threw a dead bird out of his hide *just before a passing bird disappeared over* the hedge. The flutter of this falling was a good enough imitation of a settling bird to bring in others.

Another trick which can help with pigeons is to loft a decoy up into a hedgerow tree to make it that bit more visible than those on the ground. Observation of ducks and geese shows that they are also attracted by the wing flapping of a settling bird of their own species. I have often wondered whether an enlarged version of a pigeon cradle would work for geese, and I know from experience that you can attract wigeon by using a dead bird on an ordinary pigeon flapper.

The latest piece of kit for attracting pigeons is the 'pigeon magnet'. This is a mechanical device with an electric motor which whirls its decoys (dead birds) around on the end of long arms. Having never used one I cannot offer advice from personal experience. However, I have a number of friends who have used them. Their consensus view is that the more outlandish claims of the advertisers are an overestimate, but they do pull extra birds. The thing to beware of, in particular, seems to be that incoming pigeons are frightened at the last minute, often just out of range. If you use a pigeon magnet it may well pay to switch it off once the birds are coming.

Decoy shyness

There is no doubt in my mind that birds which are regularly shot at over decoys get more and more wary of them. My best experience is with duck. On my particular Kentish marsh they will often come well early in the season, even on a still sunny day. However, most of my fellow fowlers use decoys as their prime system, and by Christmas it is clear that the birds will not look at artificial decoys on anything but a dull, and preferably breezy, day, even though they are perfectly happy to join a group of their own kind. On the other hand I have often had good success with decoys on an apparently poor day in January on areas where the local wildfowlers rarely use them. This applies even though these birds are as wild as hawks in all other respects.

Whether the same problems apply to pigeons if one uses real dead birds I am not sure. I suspect, however, that if one has really chosen a good site under the main traffic, and selected a suitably dull and breezy day, they should come well. However, if one is forced to use artificials, the type with real feathers attached will probably make an enormous difference.

Remaining hidden

Even when the sham has worked well, and the birds have decided to come to your set, you can easily blow the whole thing by being seen as you move to take a shot. Hence the emphasis earlier in this chapter on choosing a good place to hide. In most cases, however, a provident nature will not give adequate cover without a little help from you.

When you are really lucky you find yourself with a chest-deep dry ditch with rough grasses growing well on both banks to provide a face screen. Even here, however, birds crossing the ditch may well spot you as they circle to come in again, in which case a little screening on either side of you is needed.

Good hides come in a multitude of forms, but several basic rules apply to all of them. Firstly, they must be large enough to shelter both you and your dog comfortably, with room to turn round when you need to. Much less than 5ft in diameter becomes very restrictive when you try to turn and raise your gun in one manoeuvre. Secondly they must be unobtrusive. This can be achieved either by blending in to the local vegetation, or by using a familiar object. The bale hide which imitates a harmless stack of straw is a classic example. Thirdly, it pays handsomely if you can see through your hide to watch approaching birds, rather than showing your horribly pale face over the top. Another vital factor is background. It is not good having a good screen in front if you are silhouetted against the sky or water when you move to take your shot.

Most pigeon shooters will obtain permission and then use trimmings from hedges or woods to build a hide. When carefully chosen, such materials will

John Batley demonstrates hides with good and bad background. Previous page, looks good until he has to show himself for a shot, because there is not enough behind him. The smaller hide with the dropped front (above) provides plenty of cover and a good background – you hardly see him when he pops up to take a shot.

blend well with the local environment, and provide a perfect semi-transparent screen through which to peer. Another choice is to carry a bundle of forked sticks and a piece of camouflage netting to set up wherever you choose. This has one main disadvantage – you will need to know where you intend to set up when choosing the right colour of netting. Also, in a strong wind in open country, netting is apt to flap in the wind, and can scare birds which might otherwise have come in.

When using a portable hide I prefer to carry one made of rigid plastic garden netting. This rolls up easily and is held up by a few hazel rods woven into the meshes. I can then weave natural grasses and rushes into the netting to match the local environment. In practice I leave the dead vegetation on the hide at all times and find that I only have to fill in any gaps which have occurred since the last use. For most purposes the dead grass colour suits well, but if I need to use it in front of a green summer hedgerow it is easy to weave in a few twigs of fresh leaves along the top edge, leaving the lower area to match the dead grasses of the hedgebank.

I have even used this hide successfully in the middle of a stubble field by setting it up against a broken big round bale. A few handfuls of loose straw shaken over the top edge, and the match with background is superb.

Once you are in your hide, always cultivate the habit of peering through the thin screen of cover rather than over it, especially as you watch birds approach. Also, you will be much less obvious when on lookout if the back is higher than the front so that your head is not silhouetted against the skyline to anything approaching low from the front.

Section 3
MANAGING THE SHOOT

15

Conservation and Restocking Policy

'The presence of a flourishing population of wild-bred pheasants can be taken as prima facie evidence of an environment rich in natural breeding habitat, suitable nesting cover and abundant insect and plant food for young chicks and adult birds. Such an environment does not only favour wild game but will probably also be rich in a wide variety of other wildlife including songbirds, wild flowers and butterflies.'

Colin McKelvie *A Future for Game* (1985)

Good habitat

Every living organism needs a home. It is a basic truth of ecology that if a suitable habitat is not available for a particular species that species will not exist. Also, populations normally settle to what might be termed the carrying capacity of their environment. Thus, in trying to manage your shoot to enhance the population of a given quarry, your first aim must be to improve habitat quality. Taking some specific examples will help to illustrate the point.

The pheasant, our first example, is basically a bird of the woodland edge, and holding capacity for this species is governed by the quantity and quality of edge. If your shoot has just one square 10 acre wood, you will only hold the number of pheasants which can live around its edges. However, if you split the wood into four equal parts by cutting some 20 or 25 yard wide rides in the form of a cross through the wood, you will create much more edge habitat and thus increase the pheasant holding capacity. Improving the quality of the edges and ride sides will help too (see Chapter 16).

A second example is that of snipe. Many shoots have a wet corner which is rarely, if ever, visited by these birds. Snipe like to have a few small patches of open water, even if these are only a matter of a few inches across. Going into your wetland area with a spade and digging out a few sods, or blocking a ditch so that a small area floods in winter, may be all that is needed. Now your marsh has some small patches of standing water which glisten in the sun as the snipe passes overhead, so it decides to call in for a closer inspection.

This then is the first and most important key to shoot improvement. Make sure that you offer the right sort of habitat and you will automatically attract and hold more game. You will also make conditions more attractive for the resident species in the breeding season, so breeding densities may well grow up. This, in turn, should mean more game to shoot next season provided that breeding success is high, and predation is under reasonable control, of which more later.

Lastly, of course, a well-managed habitat should improve conditions for any hand-reared birds which you decide to release to supplement your shooting. This will inevitably reduce straying problems, and therefore mean a better return on your investment. All such work has a broader conservation value too (see Chapter 16).

Wild versus reared

If, once you have carried out all the habitat improvement that you can, you still do not find enough game to suit your needs, topping up the population *may* be the answer. However, releasing gamebirds should not be seen as an automatic route to better shooting. Hand-reared birds may well be poorer performers than their wild-bred counterparts in all sorts of regards.

We know, for example, that most hand-reared grey partridges in the United Kingdom have birds of Danish origin in their ancestry. These birds have clearly been selected for various characteristics which are of a desirable nature from the game farmers' point of view. Sadly, it seems that while this has been going on, adverse factors in relation to survival and breeding success in the wild have been bred in. As a result, releasing grey partridges in areas where there are still wild stocks may actually be counter productive for wild partridge conservation in the long term.

Similar problems are known with pheasants. Research at The Game Conservancy Trust has clearly shown that hand-reared hen pheasants are much less 'street wise' about predation that their wild counterparts. As a consequence, the average hand-reared hen rears only 20 per cent of the chicks which a wild bird produces. Thus, in areas where there are significant wild stocks, releasing may well cause long-term damage. Not only do the released birds left after the shooting season occupy good breeding habitat to the detriment of wild birds, but there can also be more subtle effects too. One of these is that the presence of reared birds may cause over-shooting of wild stocks. This latter situation can apply to partridges as well.

With the exception of cock pheasants, wild populations can normally only sustain a fairly low rate of cropping up to a maximum in a good year of 25 to

A good wild pheasant brood. Do not overshoot or these will be a thing of the past. *(Terence Blank)*

30 per cent of their autumn population. However, most released gamebirds are shot rather harder – after all if there are plenty of birds there, why not shoot 50 per cent more? The problem is that it is usually impossible to recognise the difference between the two stocks on shooting days, and the wild birds therefore receive the same shooting pressure. The result is an almost inevitable decline in wild stocks which means that eventually hand rearing becomes the only viable method of providing shooting.

Do we add pheasants?

From the foregoing it will be clear that it is very difficult to run a shoot in which a balance is struck between wild and hand-reared pheasants. In most cases, it is an 'either/or' situation. Either conserve wild birds, shoot gently especially in poor wild production years, and do not expect great numbers, or accept that the wild stock will not provide what you want, release birds annually, and be grateful for the extras in a year when a benevolent nature provides good breeding conditions. In practice, most shoots fall into the latter category and there is nothing wrong with this so long as they are doing the job properly. As already mentioned, woodland management for game helps many other species too, so pheasant shoots which rely mainly on hand-reared birds are still good for conservation generally, provided that they do not release ridiculous numbers of pheasants without doing anything to improve the habitat.

In the wetter western part of the United Kingdom, and particularly in country which grows little or no cereals, there is no choice anyway. If you want anything more than the very occasional pheasant, release of hand-reared birds is the only option. I hazard, indeed, that it has always been so. Even in the heyday of wild game at the turn of the century, large numbers of pheasants were reared and released to provide shooting – especially on the bigger shoots.

The important point to establish is that every shoot must decide its own policy on this question of restocking. Some opinion says that there would be almost no sport without releasing pheasants; to do so, therefore, is necessary. Other opinion wishes to keep costs to a minimum and be happy with a bag made up mainly of rabbits and pigeons, and perhaps wildfowl if they have the right habitat. There are also a few places, mainly in the drier east of the country, where wild game production is reasonable, and where good keepering and predation control are sufficient to provide all the sport that is required. Perhaps the rarest shoot of all is one which combines this approach with a little low-intensity hand rearing. Most likely this will mean keeping a small flock of traditional bantams, and using these as foster mothers for eggs picked up from badly sited or cut out nests. It is surprising how easy it is to rear up to a couple of hundred birds in this way. Also, the birds are so much more 'naturally' produced than in the normal brooder hut system, and probably much more similar in behaviour to wild birds that to hand-reared birds. This is especially so with pheasants, since the bantam foster mothers are also 'woodland' birds and therefore teach good behaviour patterns.

The value of variety
There is another question to be faced when considering whether to use hand-reared game to top up the amount of shooting available. This is whether it will change the nature of the shoot itself, and thus spoil your enjoyment of it. In any group of Guns there will always be those who are keen to add reared birds, or to rear more, so that they can have more shooting. However, once you have released a number of birds, you become almost obliged to pursue them. This is fine, indeed it would be pretty daft to release birds for shooting and then not pursue them. However, it can become such a preoccupation that the rest of the potential which the shoot offers is ignored. For instance, a boggy field which holds a few snipe might be left untouched in favour of an extra pheasant drive on the last day of the season when a good stock of pheasants is left.

For me, one of the elements which adds enormously to the quality of the day is variety. For example I once had a memorable day on a shoot based around an area of gravel pits. Dawn flight produced three species of duck and two of geese, plus a pigeon. This was followed by breakfast, and then a long morning which added pheasant, partridge, woodcock, snipe, rabbit and hare. The sweep for the day was not on the size of the bag, but the number of species.

Today, almost everyone has pheasants on their ground – they are the bread and butter gamebird for most shoots. In this circumstance, anyone who can offer variety automatically has something notable. To my mind it is sad when hand-reared pheasants or partridges become such a preoccupation that the rest of what the shoot has to offer is ignored. A few hand-reared birds can add to the day in many ways. They may be needed simply to ensure that everyone does get some shooting, and can give an opportunity to provide some really testing shots at high birds. They may also be the way to make a full day out of a shoot which otherwise only offers a morning or evening flight. All this is fine, and I certainly would not suggest that hand-reared gamebirds do not have their place. If well managed, hand-reared pheasants and partridges can provide superb sport. I do, however, feel that it is easy to spoil a good rough shoot by adding reared birds, and particularly pheasants, without considering carefully what the area already has to offer, what can be done to enhance this, and how best it can be used.

It is outside the scope of this book to describe release methods in detail, but there are a number of useful guides to releasing available, notably the Game Conservancy Trust's Guide *Gamebird Releasing* (1996). Also Ian McCall's book *Your Shoot, Gamekeeping and Management* (1990) has much to offer on this and many other aspects of shoot management.

16

Habitat Management

'Studies of radio-marked pheasants clearly show how they spend the majority of their time within 20 metres of the boundaries between woodland and open ground.'

David Hill and Peter Robertson *The Pheasant: Ecology, management and conservation* (1988)

Effective management of game and wildlife habitats is a complex subject – one about which much has been written over the years. A brief chapter such as this can therefore only provide a few pointers and basic ideas. Anyone who feels the need for more information is strongly advised to consult more specialist publications, or better still, expert advisors in the field. The Game Conservancy Trust, for example, can provide both a visiting consultancy service on all aspects of shoot management, and a series of guidebooks which form a back-up to this service.

In the long run, good advice is cheap, and lack of it can lead to expensive mistakes being made, as well as possible environmental damage.

Improving the woods

Most woodland work will be aimed at improving conditions for pheasants, although a fortunate few landowners may have woodcock as the prime game species. Fortuitously the basic requirements of the two birds are similar, so most work will help both at once.

In the quest for maximum timber production, foresters are apt to plant timber trees right to the edge of the wood. As the wood grows up this results in a steep edge, with overhanging branches, and very little cover at ground level. The shade cast by overhanging trees means that any shrubby species which grow at the edge are thin and straggly as they shoot up in search of better light conditions.

This lack of good shrub cover has very important consequences for pheasants. Remember that they are basically pedestrian birds which therefore spend the majority of the daylight hours on the ground. Remember, too, that they are birds of the woodland edge. With the wood edge structure described above there is absolutely nothing to stop the wind whistling in at ground level. As a consequence the critical 20 yards or so which should be used most by the pheasants are cold and draughty.

The correct edge structure is a reverse of the one described, with good cover at ground level, and nothing above. Thicker cover at a greater height then becomes significant as one moves into the wood. The perfect wood edge therefore starts with a good, well-managed and regularly trimmed hedge which keeps the wind out at ground level. Inside this one should find an area of shrubby cover, scrub or coppice of gradually increasing height and then, finally, the first of the forest trees. The overall effect is of a wood edge which slopes up and in at about 45 degrees, so that even the outer hedge on a north face receives full sunlight on a summer's day. This also has the effect of gently funnelling the wind upwards, and producing much better shelter than a solid vertical edge. As a result, pheasants within the wood find comfortable draught-free accommodation both during the daytime and when roosting in the trees at night.

Quantity of edge is important too. Once woods exceed a few acres or so in size, they become large enough, unless in the form of very long narrow belts, to have central areas which are comparatively rarely used by pheasants. This can be at least partially remedied by cutting wide rides within the wood. If carefully designed, such rides can improve holding capacity, provide brood-rearing areas, and make useful gunstands which help in showing the birds. To be really effective in this way, a ride will need to be about 50 yards or more wide, with shrubby edges giving the same kind of sloped effect as the outside of the wood. Research carried out by The Game Conservancy Trust has shown that from a territory formation point of view pheasants do not consider rides narrower than this as a woodland edge. However, any sort of ride is better than none at all both from the winter holding cover and the general conservation points of view.

Cutting such wide rides in large woods can be a major undertaking, well outside the scope of the small rough shoot. However, creating small openings in the woodland canopy is much easier, and also beneficial to game. It is too often true to say that woods have suffered from neglect and lack of management over the last few decades. As a consequence, shrub and ground cover has declined as the woodland canopy has closed, leaving a cold bare woodland floor which is unattractive to game and indeed most other wildlife.

Cutting a skylight around 25 to 30 yards wide is within the capabilities of a couple of people with a chainsaw, and is often all that is needed to encourage new growth from dormant bramble and other shrubs once the sunlight penetrates to the woodland floor. You should obviously take care to choose your site so that you do not need to cut any large forest trees. However, most semi-natural woods will have areas of birch, hazel, ash and similar species which have grown up rapidly but do not present too many huge trunks.

If you wish to cut any significant volume of timber which is above 10cm (4in) in diameter at breast height you will need to consult the Forestry Commission to obtain a felling licence. To fail to do so is to break the law, except for the small allowance of up to 5 cubic metres per quarter (provided that not more than 2 cubic metres are sold) for the landowner's private use. This amounts to no more than one or two trees, and is designed to prevent wholesale damage to the United Kingdom's landscape. Give a good reason for what you wish to do and a licence will usually be forthcoming anyway.

You should also take care over the question of conservation value. If your wood is a Site of Special Scientific Interest (SSSI), felling of timber will be one of the many 'potentially damaging operations' which could occur. As a result, you are required by law to consult English Nature, Scottish Natural Heritage or the Countryside Council for Wales depending on where you live, before work begins. Again, do not be afraid to do so. If what you propose is seen as likely to either cause no harm, or to be good for the wood, the relevant body will agree a management plan, and be pleased that you are interested in the conservation of your wood.

Managing the hedges

The cover offered by hedges, ditches and fence lines often provides a major part of the rough shooter's sport. These narrow strips of shelter are easily hunted by just one or two Guns and a dog. They can hold an enormous array of game; pheasant, partridge, duck, woodcock, snipe, rabbit, hare and pigeon are all flushed from such places at times. They are also a habitat feature over which the ordinary rough shooter can hope to have some influence.

It is well known that in the quest for increased farm efficiency many miles of hedgerow have been removed since the end of the Second World War. What is less well known is that the quality of many existing hedges has declined too. A combination of reduced management and accidental damage means that many hedges are but a shadow of their former selves.

One of the worst problems has been spray drift from neighbouring fields. This has often resulted in a gradual destruction of the herb communities which grow in the hedge bottom, with a resultant decline in their value as game and wildlife cover. Just to add insult to injury, this can often provide a good habitat for more invasive weed species, which become a problem for the farmer as they spread out into his crop.

The Game Conservancy Trust is hard at work researching how to rectify this problem, so that we can see a return to wildlife-rich hedgerows which provide

Hedges need active management if game and wildlife are to thrive. *(The Game Conservancy Trust)*

good nesting cover for game without presenting a serious problem to the farmer. Part of the answer is the adoption of a narrow 'sterile strip' between the hedge and crop to prevent invasion by weeds, since as time goes on the invasive species will usually die out due to natural succession if spray drift ceases. A good contribution to prevention of spray drift problems is the use of The Game Conservancy Trust's conservation headland technique (see Chapter 8).

Alongside this, hedges need active management if they are to provide the best results for the shoot. A good hedge should be windproof at ground level, which means regular trimming to keep it low and thick. In practice a thorough trimming every second year seems to be the best choice. Annual trimming can result in a shortage of nesting cover in the spring, but is far better than leaving the hedge too long between cutting. Whatever happens, however, do not mow the bank below. The herb cover of the hedge base is essential in the spring as nesting sites. If your farmer is over-zealous in this regard, volunteering to do the job for him may be the answer.

Where hedges have been let go, more drastic measures are needed. The skills involved in cutting and laying outgrown hedges are worth learning, and local farmers' training groups often hold hedge laying courses. Once the hedge is back in shape, regular trimming should keep it in good order to the benefit of both farm and shoot. However, hedges can easily be ruined by livestock. Sheep in particular can cause enormous damage by grazing out everything at the base of the hedge, especially at the high stocking densities which are used on modern farms. Such damage can be prevented using the modern, cheap and easily handled electric fencing systems which make hedgerow protection much easier than in times past. Few sheep rearing enterprises would be without such equipment these days anyway. It is not that time consuming to erect an electric fence to protect your hedges. It really is rather irresponsible not to do this in today's conservation conscious age. If you rent the shooting, and your farmer cannot be bothered, you might offer to help him by setting the fence up. With luck it will prick his conscience for the future.

Open country

May people equate conservation with planting something, and well-planned tree and shrub planting can be a huge benefit. However, there is much more to conservation than just sticking in some trees. Also, in some areas it can be positively counter-productive.

Trees are good for woodland wildlife, but all species do not live in woods. Some wildlife thrives in open country without trees. Grey partridges are a classic example. In choosing nest sites they positively avoid hedgerows with trees. This is a basic instinct which probably tells them that trees can be dangerous as lookout posts for birds of prey.

Many other species like open country too. Lapwings, stone curlews, skylarks, corn buntings, harvest mice and hares are all basically grassland species. They have adapted well to arable farming, and provided that it is done sensitively they can thrive.

So, if you have the good fortune to shoot over a piece of open partridge country with hedges and ditches, do not rush to plant trees. To conserve your partridges, and the other open country wildlife, think in terms of splitting some of the bigger fields with grass banks (The Game Conservancy Trust's beetle bank technique). Also, look to imaginative use of set-aside, and perhaps conservation headlands (see Chapter 8) to provide brood-rearing habitat and enhance game production.

Marshes and ponds

Wetland management is perhaps the most complex habitat question faced by the rough shooter, and the importance of seeking good advice is therefore great. A few brief thoughts on the most common questions is really all that can be covered in this book.

The main scope for the inland fowler is surface-feeding duck such as mallard, teal and wigeon. These are all birds of shallow waters – almost, in

Grading the edges to provide more shallows on a flight pool. *(Ian McCall, The Game Conservancy Trust)*

fact, the water's edge. This means that, just as with pheasants and woods, amount and quality of habitat is the key factor. If you have a small, round, steep-sided pool over which to flight your birds, the obvious trick is to change the shape and in the process grade the edges to a more gentle slope.

Given use of a digging machine for a day, it should be possible to draw out one or two shallow bays, at the same time using some of the spoil to build up the adjacent pond bed and create further shallows. By doing this both the length of edge and its quality can be enhanced.

Having either improved a pool in this way, or dug a new one, many people are keen to plant it up as soon as possible. This is hardly surprising – a new pool means a lot of bare earth which looks as though it needs blending into the landscape. However, it is easy to overdo the planting. The naturally occurring rushes and rough grasses which grow up around a pool are likely to provide ideal wildfowl habitat without human assistance. The most important aspect is to leave a reasonable margin of about 10 yards or so around the water, and to keep livestock out. If the pool *must* be used for livestock watering it is best to fence them out from most of it and provide a narrow corridor to the water. The fence should extend well out into the water too, or else form a complete loop, otherwise the stock will eventually get at the valuable bankside vegetation from the inside.

Trees which are planted too close to a pool can be very damaging. As they grow up they cast shade over the waterside vegetation and reduce its productivity. Also, if the canopy reaches out too far it becomes difficult for duck to flight in. If you feel the need to add bushes and trees around your pool, do so well back from the waters' edge. The combined effect can then be of a good area of mixed habitat which holds both gamebirds and duck.

Marshes and water meadows pose other problems, and sweeping generalisations about how to manage them are very dangerous. In most cases their value lies largely in the 'status quo'. They will usually have evolved over a very long period, and their wildfowl populations will be a reflection of past management. As a general statement, the best marshes simply require maintenance of their traditional management to retain their value. One of the greatest disasters that can befall an area of natural water meadows is a sudden change in the grazing regime. Maintain the livestock at the traditional levels and you will be most likely to maintain the wildfowl habitat in good order. Fencing out stock can be as damaging as over-grazing. Similarly, cessation of pollarding or of reed cutting for thatch can lead to the habitat becoming too enclosed for wildfowl.

Correct drainage is important too. Deep ditching with modern machinery can be very damaging if it leads to excessive drying out. On the other hand, some drainage of marshes which have traditionally been hand ditched may be essential. Many rich meadow systems have reverted to comparatively uniform and sterile reed swamps in the absence of any drainage.

Wetlands are ecological systems which are often in a state of continuous change. Regular low-key maintenance is usually the way to maximize wildlife diversity and to create the best in wildfowl value. Over-development and total neglect are often as dangerous as each other.

Conservation and game management

From what has gone before it becomes abundantly clear that good shoot management has much to offer in broader conservation terms. All who shoot know this anyway. But, are you well versed in all the arguments? If not, you should hang your head in shame – and get clued up. In the end, paying your subscriptions to the field sports organisations is not enough. Membership of The Game Conservancy Trust, BASC, The Countryside Alliance and so on is only part of the story. No matter how hard they try, these organisations cannot do the job alone.

Everyone who shoots has it in his power to influence others, even if it is only the regulars at the dart board in the local. They all have the right to vote, and they *could* all vote against us if there were a referendum on the future of shooting.

You should not expect to convert rabid antis into keen shooters. Killing for sport, or pleasure, or whatever you wish to call it, is a moral question. Many people may well find it morally unacceptable for themselves. Arguments about morality are apt to get nowhere. If you have read this far you have obviously sorted out the moral question for yourself, probably on the basis that you get enormous satisfaction and enjoyment from your shooting, and that you do not believe that you are doing any harm either to your fellow man or to your chosen quarry species. This is fine, and good, and is really the right point to leave unproductive moral argument and move on to a different tack.

If you will take my advice, the tack to move on to is conservation. Explain to your audience the good which fieldsports do, both for the quarry themselves, and for the other species of flora and fauna which inhabit their environment. You must, however, *be sure of your ground*. Airy-fairy general statements are likely to be spotted for what they are. Do not just say 'We release lots of birds, so we are helping populations.' As has already been made clear, releasing may not help, and conservationists know this.

The argument of enlightened self-interest is sound, however. It goes along the lines of 'I want to show the pleasure of this wonderful sport to my grand-children. I and others like me have an enormous vested interest in maintaining our chosen quarry and its habitat.' It is a fact that those with the greatest interest in anything are those with a self-interest. Wildfowlers fight fervently to protect the wonderful wetlands against pollution, development, and a multi-tude of other threats, alongside the other conservation interests. They know their ground at least as well as other users by the simple truth of needing to if they are to enjoy their sport to the full. They also have the practical skills to be able to work on maintenance and improvement. The simple truth of this is illustrated, for example, by the fact that the Dorset Wildfowlers are one of the most important groups involved in the regular Poole Harbour clean-ups. They have the boats and the navigation skills to collect rubbish from the salt-ings and waters. The other volunteers can only pick up along the strand line.

One of the great public relations exercises of shooting sports followed the 1954 Protection Of Birds Act. This was the principle promoted by WAGBI of returning something to balance for what was taken. Tens of thousands of ducks were reared by wildfowlers, to be released onto unshot reserves where they would enhance wild populations. It looked good, and it was good, but not for the immediately obvious reason. To understand this we must understand the results of recent research into the way in which hand-reared birds acclimatise.

As mentioned earlier (Chapter 15), we have clear evidence from The Game Conservancy Trust's research that hand-reared partridges and pheasants are nothing like so effective as contributors to the wild population as their naturally-reared brethren. There are indications at least, that hand-reared ducks leave a lot to be desired. They seem to nest in silly places, and often start to lay so early in the new year that any ducklings which hatch have little chance of

Mallard for release on an unshot reserve. The reserve is in many senses more valuable than the ducks put onto it.

survival in the prevailing cold conditions. Add to this the fact that increased populations rapidly fall back over a few years to the carrying capacity of their environment and you begin to realise the long-term futility of hand rearing as a means of conserving *wild* populations. Hand rearing is basically a technique to provide a short-term increase in the numbers of birds available for shooting – and perfectly reasonable if not taken to excess. However, in itself, it is not conservation.

The great benefits of the WAGBI hand-rearing programme were two. First, all the birds were ringed prior to release. As a consequence we now know much more about migration, movement, and population dynamics of mallard than we might. The other, even greater, benefit was the unshot reserves. To ensure the safety of their birds, the clubs took on the management and improvement of ponds and marshes on which to release their birds. As a consequence the quality of our wetlands as a whole was enhanced much more than many people realise. That good work continues – with more clubs than ever managing wetlands today.

This is but a small part of the conservation story, however. Apart from flight ponds, wildfowlers have little power to create new wetlands. They can only really hope to conserve what we have. However, game shooters can, and do, have much more effect. By sheer weight of numbers they are more significant anyway, and inland game shooting often involves investment of more in financial terms. This means there is much more resource available for conservation. Woods, spinneys, hedges, and game crops are all maintained or even planted by inland shooters while moors and marshes are actively managed. These areas are spread over the whole countryside and amount to a far greater area than nature reserves.

The list of good works is almost endless, and a couple of examples will have to suffice. One of the most widely known is heather moorland. It is a fact that much of the United Kingdom's heather upland survives because of grouse shooting. Where grouse are actively conserved, heather is conserved too, and with it comes a whole range of upland species from cloudberry to merlins. Once an interest in grouse is lost, grazing pressure goes up, heather is reduced or eliminated, and as the moor becomes less productive, even for sheep, its use is changed to extensive softwood forestry. Since non-native trees are usually used, and in monoculture at that, the result is a scenic and conservation disaster.

Another good example is given by woodland management for pheasants. So many of our lowland woods are gradually declining in diversity, due to the uneconomic nature of management. Hurdle making has all but disappeared, and with it, hazel coppicing. The result is cold, bare and draughty woods which are as poor for game as for wildlife. However, The Game Conservancy Trust research has shown that pheasant releasing is a major incentive for improved management. Shooters who wish to hold their birds well, and provide better sport for themselves get coppice rotations going again, open up wide rides, and plant native species. All of this helps woodland diversity enormously. One specific example is given by butterflies in oak and hazel woods. Given no management, such woods often only hold three or four species, and for every mile that you walk on a sunny day you will only see two or three butterflies. Take a look along wide rides that have been cut for pheasant shooting in the same kind of wood – you will find not four, but 19 species, and upwards of 90 individuals per mile walked. Other groups such as songbirds benefit too, but so far it has not been easy to quantify this.

Thus, next time you are attacked by an anti, turn the tables on him. Ask him to name a quarry species which is in decline because of shooting. Then point out that they are all thriving, and that this is because of, rather than in spite of shooting. Add the benefits to other species too, and you find that shooting is actually a major tool for the good of conservation generally. The BASC slogan 'Always been Green' says it all.

17

Predation Control

'So, in late February or March, weather permitting, start your trap line when the enemies of game are hungry and moving around. And carry on as late as you can. Do not forget the old maxim, 'The trap works while the keeper sleeps'; so very true since most of these creatures operate at night.'

Archie Coats *The Amateur Keeper* (1962)

Lack of good habitat management is not the only reason why wild game populations are often low as we learned earlier (see Chapter 15). Predators can be an important factor too, and may well be a serious component in preventing a resurgence of game when habitat is improved. However, it is fair to say that game management has a bad name in some conservation circles because gamekeepers are widely held to have been responsible for the near extinction in the last century of some of our rarest birds and beasts of prey. This, plus the continued and unbelievably stupid use of illegal or indiscriminate methods of control, such as poisoning and pole trapping, means that any form of predator control is a bitter pill for the conservationist to swallow. It is therefore essential for all who wish to control predators as an aid to game management to understand both the legal situation and the justification for control.

Why control predators?
There is no doubt that a wide range of predator species eat game as part of their diet. This alone might be considered good reason for control, but responsible game managers should be asking, 'Is this predation significant?' If it is not, there is no sense in control. One important scientific study on this is the work which was carried out by The Game Conservancy Trust during the 1980s on Salisbury Plain. This has shown that wild partridge populations are very

much influenced by predation. For instance, 58 per cent of the partridge pairs on one area during 1989 produced no young even though they survived themselves. The indication was that they lost their clutches, probably repeatedly, to avian predators such as crows and magpies. Add this to a further 20 per cent of the pairs in which the hen disappeared too – no doubt killed on the nest by ground predators – and you have a partridge population in serious decline due to the effects of predation alone.

Which predators cause most damage?

Different game species can suffer significant predation at different times in their life cycle. Thus, for example, those shoots whose sport is reliant on hand-reared pheasants alone, will not suffer nest predation problems due to magpies. It is a simple fact that magpies are not able to kill birds as large as pheasant poults under normal circumstances, and that they are therefore very unlikely to try. However, ground predators such as mink, fox, stoat and rat can all take pheasant poults at release time and could well have an effect on shooting. On the other hand, wild partridges will be far enough forward at this time of year that predation is largely irrelevant. In their case it is the effects of both nest robbers and ground predators in spring that is important.

The major game predators can be split into two groups, avian and ground.

Avian predators

All owls, hawks, falcons and other raptors are protected in the United Kingdom. Thus, even if they do affect game, it is illegal even to attempt to kill or take them.

This leaves two groups of predatory birds which may be controlled: some gulls and some members of the crow family. Both groups may be taken throughout the year. However, with a few minor exceptions, which do not really affect the rough shooter, the only methods allowed are shooting or cage trapping. Also, The Wildlife and Countryside Act, 1981 provides that they may only be taken by authorised persons. This, in effect, means the land-owner, the holder of the sporting rights, or persons specifically permitted by them to do so.

The gulls which may be controlled in this way are the herring, lesser black-backed and greater black-backed. All other gulls are protected. While these species do not pose problems on most areas, they can be very significant predators in some circumstances. One example is the case of a breeding colony living near a wildfowl breeding area. They may not actively hunt for ducks' nests, but they will take both eggs and ducklings, and sheer weight of numbers can impose an intolerable strain on the wildfowl.

In the case of the crow family, five species may be taken: magpie, crow (carrion and hooded), rook, jackdaw and jay. Ravens and choughs are fully protected. All five species can be serious predators of game eggs, but crows and magpies in particular make deliberate searches for nests. These two species are therefore the most important to control.

Control of these predatory birds by shooting is likely to be only a partial answer, since the corvids especially are very wary. They rarely come into shotgun range unless the gunner is well hidden. However, those who carry a gun on their rounds should be able to account for a significant number in the course of a year. Rifles offer a much longer range, and the lightest bullet weights with .22 centre fire calibres can be particularly valuable because of their very flat trajectory and the low risk of a ricochet. A well-hidden marksman with a good rest can often pick off a crow or magpie at 100 yards or more before it even realises that it is in any danger. As with all rifle shooting, a good safe background is essential – do not squeeze the trigger unless you are sure of safety.

Cage trapping is a much neglected technique which can account for large numbers of corvids. Multi-catch cages with funnel entrances work on the lobster pot principle and can be particularly effective against flock-living birds. One of the keys to success is to pre-bait with the roof off until the birds have

Look out for footprints in the mud. If you are lucky you may get an early warning that there is a fox about.

overcome their suspicion and become regular users of the cage. Large numbers may then be caught in a single day. Many users recommend that the trap should not be emptied until after dark, to avoid scaring those still outside. The normal practice is then to return to pre-baiting until another large group is coming regularly for the food.

Such traps are unfortunately of little use against crows and magpies in the spring, when most become territorial. Since this is the season when they do the most damage to wild game interests, control is essential. The Game Conservancy Trust pioneered the use of the larsen trap in the late 1980s. This is a small cage with sprung doors and a live caller bird. This method can be dramatically effective from mid-March to early June. The welfare of the live caller is of paramount importance to success, however, and it is essential to give it sufficient room to stretch its wings freely. It also needs shelter, a perch and a regular supply of food and clean water. These are legal requirements anyway, but an active and healthy caller is far more effective in its decoy role.

Ground predators

In most areas, the main mammalian predator of game is the fox, with the smaller ground predators such as mink, stoat, weasel, rat and grey squirrel taking second place. Feral cats should also be mentioned as a potentially serious problem but the Scottish wild cat is now fully protected by the Wildlife and Countryside Act, as are the pine marten, the badger and the otter. It is also important to remember that domestic cats are considered property and therefore protected by the Theft Act, even when they take to hunting the hedgerows for game in their spare time. The keeper is only legally able to kill a truly feral cat.

Mink, stoat, weasel, rat, grey squirrel and feral cats may all be killed at all times, although control methods are limited to shooting, trapping and snaring except in the case of the rat and the grey squirrel, which may be killed with specifically approved poisons. The rat may also be gassed using legally approved phosphine products phostoxin and talunex.

Two other species which may cause problems are given partial protection by The Wildlife and Countryside Act. These are the hedgehog, which quite often takes eggs, and can even on occasions take pheasant poults in a release pen, and the polecat which can be quite as destructive as the mink. Both these species may be shot, but no trapping or snaring is allowed.

Fox control

While the fox is generally the most important predator of lowland game, the damage is likely to be seasonal, and going after foxes outside of the damage season is largely a waste of time. This is because creating a space only invites new colonists to move in, with the result that you still have to kill foxes during the damage season to have any real effect. The two periods when low ground game is particularly vunerable are during the nesting season, and in the case of naïve released poults, the immediately post release period. Therefore, shooting foxes during the game shooting season is largely a waste of time, as well as being unpopular on safety grounds on many shoots.

This is not to say that the shotgun is not a useful weapon for fox control. Carefully organised drives can be very effective. The key to success is to know your covert well, and know the likely exit routes for 'Charlie'. By placing well hidden Guns downwind of these places, and having one or two 'beaters' approaching quietly from upwind it is often possible to be highly successful at gently moving foxes in such a way as to produce easy and safe shots, at relatively close range. Too much noise is distinctly unhelpful, in that foxes are much more likely to panic and run, making them much harder to kill.

Well set tunnel traps can account for many game predators. *(The Game Conservancy Trust)*

Today, increasing numbers of people are turning to night control of foxes using calls and shooting with a high powered rifle. This is an efficient and very humane system, but it does require considerable skill and a thorough understanding of the safe use of rifles. The other main method of control is the snare. This is also very effective, but again needs considerable care. It is important to remember that all self-locking snares are now illegal, and that all snares must be checked each day. Great care must be taken to avoid any risk to non-target species such as badgers or deer, both of which it is illegal to snare.

Smaller ground predators

Mink, stoat, weasel, rat or grey squirrel are all species which can kill game. Indeed the mink could vie with the fox as the most serious game predator in some areas. Grey squirrels are probably the least important on the list, but even they will take eggs, as well as stealing food put out for game and damaging growing trees in game coverts. All five species can be taken in tunnel traps using any one of the legally approved spring traps. It is important to remember that the trap must fit well back into the tunnel for safety reasons, and that the tunnel width and height should give just enough room for the trap to spring freely and no more. Most keepers improve the safety by restricting the tunnel entrance with a couple of sticks.

Mink may also be taken in specially designed cage traps set alongside watercourses. They are curious animals, so anything which looks like a dark and mysterious hole is likely to be investigated. Remember that, with very minor exceptions the law requires that all traps and snares must be checked at least once each day. More frequent checking is advisable anyway, both from the humane point of view, and because traps which are rapidly re-set after a capture may well catch again.

Careful and well thought out predation control programmes are of great benefit to game, but all who control predators must understand that breaches of the law are a constant threat to game shooting. Anyone who breaks the law risks bringing the whole of shooting into disrepute, and stands condemned by all true sportsmen.

Active rough shooters will often get a shot at a predator as they tour their ground. They are therefore apt to assume that they have things under reasonable control by shooting alone. This is in fact rarely true. Trapping repays the time and investment involved handsomely, and can be a fascinating art in itself which gives much enjoyment at a time of year when the rough shooter is otherwise much less active than during the main winter shooting season.

18

Continuing Care

'Modern farms and woods can prove to be hungry habitats for game and wildlife in winter.'

Ian McCall *Your Shoot: Gamekeepering and Management* (1985)

Enjoying a successful rough shoot is not just a case of turning up every once in a while with dog and gun and sallying forth to shoot what you can find. To get the fullest enjoyment out of your sport you should be prepared to invest some effort into seeing that there will be game to shoot. Gathering some of the fruits of one's own labours is even sweeter in many regards than just exploiting the wilderness. The best rough shoots are the places where people look after the habitat, control the predators, and see to it that the game is cared for.

Leaving a healthy stock
The question of overshooting and its effects on wild game has been raised a number of times, but it is as well to draw things together. In an age when most lowland game is hand reared, getting a 'good return' which is better than the national average of 40 per cent is considered a measure of a shoot's success, but should this be the prime aim? I am afraid I do not think so. The real end should surely be, to quote Ian Pitman's words at the start of this book '. . . the pursuit of that truer happiness . . .'

   If this is indeed the case then the size of the bag is not particularly important, and the percentage at the end of the season is even less so. The key is rather to have shot a few memorable birds, enjoyed a few meals of game, and to know that you are a force for good in the countryside rather than the reverse. So, I say again, please do not be greedy. Take your fair share by all means, but do not eat into the seed corn.

Do not forget to provide for your birds in the harsh weather of winter. *(Ian McCall, The Game Conservancy Trust)*

Food in winter

Harsh winter weather can be a real test for much of our wildlife. Deep snow in particular makes life hard for ground-feeding birds like pheasants or partridges. Those shoots who release birds will have a feeding system in operation anyway, if they expect to hold on to any of their avian investment. This is a complex subject, and some useful guides are listed in the bibliography. Even those who are reliant on truly wild game will be wise to help out with a little grub at the harshest times. A few handfuls of corn scattered in areas regularly frequented by coveys of partridges; a bale split open and scattered, with the addition of some wheat for pheasants – these things are not hard to arrange, and they can make all the difference to how well your birds survive, and how fit they are come nesting time. Indeed, you should not forget that wild gamebirds are just as likely to stray as reared ones if they are not well fed.

The issue of being in good condition at breeding time has come to the fore in the late 1990s. Research by The Game Conservancy Trust has shown that provision of food after the shooting season is much more critical than we had

The stuff that dreams are made of. A good mixed bag that would make anyone's season.
(John Marchington)

supposed. Comparative trials between unfed areas and places where food is provided until the end of May have shown that pheasants on fed sites produce twice as many chicks per hen. They are also likely to be in much better condition when their chicks hatch, so that they make better mothers.

Compared to winter feeding, the technique is rather different. By the spring pheasants have moved out of the woods and established breeding territories along woodland edges, hedgerows, ditches and other similar cover. By putting a hopper every hundred yards or so along such edge habitat, and filling it with wheat, you provide a calorie top-up exactly where the birds need it. This makes for much better productivity even from that notoriously poor mother, the left-over reared hen pheasant.

Flight pond feeding has been covered earlier in some detail (see Chapter 12). However, a supplementary note is not out of place. This, again, relates to cold conditions. It is now well known that during prolonged spells of hard weather there are statutory bans on wildfowling. This applies to all duck and geese (plus woodcock, snipe, golden plover, coot and moorhen), even hand-reared birds on your own pond, if you have them.

Please do *not* cease feeding your flight ponds if the weather goes cold and you are prevented from shooting. The birds need more help then than at any other time, and it will help to re-establish flights quickly once the ban is lifted. If, as usually happens, the ban comes at the end of the season, you should still continue to feed. Indeed, a little grub supplied through February and March will help your birds to return to their breeding grounds in good fettle. This is surely a small price to pay for the sport which you have had. It will also be likely to encourage them to return early to your hospitality next season, and to bring their young with them as well.

Joining the crowd

Rough shooters and wildfowlers tend to be loners compared to the driven game shot. They come together less easily than most, but with the ever growing threats to the future of sporting shooting, come together they must. All rough shooters really should be members of the British Association for Shooting and Conservation, The Countryside Alliance and The Game Conservancy Trust (see Appendix I). As one who works for the latter organisation I might be accused of beating the drum. My answer is that I was a member of the first two organisations long before I took this job, and that the only reason for not belonging to the third was that I did not know what it was until I applied.

Suffice it to say here that the greater their resources, the more they can do to defend our right to shoot, and to ensure that there is game to shoot at.

Involvement in shooting live quarry actually implies a conservation awareness. If you are not enthralled by the wildlife which you pursue it surely cannot be worth the trouble. You do not do it for the meat alone because it would be cheaper and far easier to buy. You also do not do it just because you enjoy firing your gun. If that was all there was to it, clays would be enough. If you stick to rough shooting, it will be for the enjoyment of the whole thing. The main sport may well be concentrated into a few brief autumn and winter months, but the shooter's involvement goes on throughout the year. True sportsmen will have next year as much in mind as this. If we value our sport properly we must take on the responsibilities too. If we do not we can hardly expect to hand on a healthy countryside and healthy sport to future generations. King George VI said it so well in his famous quote, which heads *Shooting Times* every week:

'The wildlife of today is not ours to dispose of as we please. We have it in trust. We must account for it to those who come after.'

Appendix I
The Fieldsports Organisations

In today's increasingly urban society fieldsports are under growing pressure from those who object on moral grounds. Some people are totally against any form of exploitation of animals, while others seem able to resolve the moral dilemma of eating farmed meat which has been killed by someone else, but cannot hold with the idea of killing their own from the wild.

If fieldsports are to continue as a healthy part of our heritage we must be strong in their defence on both moral and scientific grounds. At present there are a number of national fieldsports organisations who are involved in this work, although there are other groups whose work is more heavily involved in the right to own guns. The main organisations have been mentioned in various places in the text of this book, but it is as well to summarise the work of each here too.

The British Association for Shooting and Conservation (BASC)

No one who carries a gun for sporting purposes should do so without joining the BASC. The Association, which has its origins in the Wildfowlers' Association, is the governing body of wildfowling and rough shooting. It works tirelessly for the defence of our sport from any sort of threat. It also publishes a number of codes of practice for the various shooting sports.

Membership brings automatic third-party liability insurance, without which no one should shoot anyway. All wildfowlers and rough shooters should support the BASC conservation and research programme; in particular by sending wings from any ducks which they shoot to the Association to assist in the BASC surveys of annual production rates.

Address: BASC, Marford Mill, Rossett, Wrexham, Clwyd, LL12 0HL. Tel. 01244 573000. www.basc.org.uk

The Countryside Alliance (CA)

The CA has a wider remit in the defence of all fieldsports. It is also active in fighting the countryman's corner on wider rural issues. Many shooting people are apt to adopt an 'I'm all right, Jack' attitude when the anti-fieldsport organisations attack fox or stag hunting, without considering which sport would be next in line if hunting were lost. The CA deserves your support even if you do not hunt. It also offers third-party liability insurance as an automatic benefit of membership.

Address: Countryside Alliance, The Old Town Hall, 367 Kennington Road, London, SE11 4PT. Tel. 0207 840 9274. www.countryside-alliance.org

The Game Conservancy Trust

The third organisation with a direct interest in shooting is The Game Conservancy Trust. This is a research and advisory organisation with a rather different remit. In simple terms the BASC and CA exist to defend our right to shoot, while The Game Conservancy Trust is there to ensure that our quarry flourishes so that there is something to shoot. At present, research is being carried out on all aspects of game ecology, with particular emphasis on trying to resolve the effects of increasingly intensive country-side management on game and wildfowl populations. The Game Conservancy Trust has always had a strong emphasis on ensuring that the results of its work are available to those who can use it to the benefit of game. With this in mind there is a visiting consultancy service which is available to all shoots, so that advice can be tailored to the specific needs of the ground concerned. The cost of a visit may seem high to the small rough shoot with a limited budget, but the potential to save needless expense and wasted effort is high too, not to mention the value which is likely to accrue through better quality sport.

Address: The Game Conservancy Trust, Fordingbridge, Hants, SP6 1EF. Tel. 01425 652381. www.gct.org.uk

The National Gamekeepers Organisation (NGO).

The NGO was formed in the late 1990s. Having amalgamated with the much older Moorland Gamekeepers Association, this group has become a leading force in promoting the professional gamekeeper as a custodian of the land. It works to support and defend the interests of both full and part-time keepers and deserves the support of all who shoot. If you are an amateur keeper, the fact that yours is only a rough shoot should not prevent you from joining as a supporter member, for all game management must be done with professionalism, even by amateurs.

Address: NGO, P.O. Box 107, Bishop Auckland, DL13 5YU. Tel. 01388 718502. www.nationalgamekeepers.org.uk

Appendix II
The Quarry in Death

Respect for the quarry and the sport which it offers has been an abiding theme throughout this book. However, once the bird and beast comes to hand, do not lose sight of its continued value. In many senses, we British are less than our European fellows at this point. They lay the bag out with full honours at the end of the day, while we just bundle it and dogs together in the boot of the car and head for home.

So, please pause for a moment and admire the bag. Treat it with the reverence which it deserves, and do your best to see that it becomes the best quality food which it has the potential to offer. Every single quarry species which is described in this book is eminently edible, and most are utterly delicious. I write from experience; I have eaten them all.

How you handle the game from the moment it comes to hand will have an enormous effect on how well it eats in due course. All shot game should be allowed to cool as quickly as possible, as its own body heat is quite enough to fuel a rapid fermentation and putrefaction which renders it inedible. Birds which are bundled together in a bag help to keep one another hot, hence the net to allow air circulation on the front of most game bags. So, if you are shooting from a hide, lay your birds out individually as they are gathered. If you lay them on their backs, the wings tend to fall part open and allow more air to circulate. If you are on the move, the spoils will have to go into your bag, but you should be able to spread them when you return to the car for lunch. If you are out all day, just take them out of your bag when you stop for lunch, and spread them out. You may only stop for twenty minutes, but even this time will allow some cooling off.

When you get home at the end of the day, hang your spoils up in a cool, well ventilated flyproof larder or outhouse. Traditionally birds are hung up by the head, and ground game by the hind legs, and all save rabbits, are hung with the the guts still in. Rabbits should be paunched as soon as possible to avoid deterioration. Personally, I also remove the digestive tract from grazing wildfowl such as wigeon and geese if I suspect that they have had their gut punctured by shot.

How long you hang your game for will be heavily influenced by personal fancy, and also by weather. It is true to say that anything which is gutted will tend to go off quite quickly compared with an intact body. However, since this strategy only applies to rabbits and wildfowl, this is not a serious problem, as most people prefer not to hang these too long.

Graphic detail on dressing and cooking your bag would be out of place here, but I would like to add one more point: I have found that presenting clean oven-ready packages for the kitchen and freezer helps domestic relations, if you do not cook for yourself. Make a point of doing the job well and your return with fresh game will be welcomed. Clean well-presented game also cooks more attractively, and eats better, than blood stained bedraggled carcasses.

There are many excellent cookery books available on game cookery, (see Bibliography). I would, however, go so far as to recommend the excellent *The Poacher's Cookbook* by Prue Coats. It has recipes for game and much more, and is full of the most delicious things imaginable.

Bon appetit.

Bibliography

Fieldsports are such individual pastimes that they always seem to have attracted people who wished to communicate to others their enthusiasm for their particular pursuit. As a result we have a tremendous heritage of fine writing telling us how, where, when, and what happened. On a dark winter's night when you cannot actually be out with your gun, there is not much to beat settling down by the fire with a dram and a good book on shooting. Every author has seen the sport through different eyes, so every one has something different to relate.

Here follows a list of some books which I have read, and found particularly interesting, useful or satisfying. The list is arranged in a sort of subject order, which is unfair, because many fall across boundaries anyway. It is also far from exhaustive, but I hope it will lead you into pleasant reading and new insights.

Quarry Identification
Braun, B. and Singer, A., *The Hamlyn Guide to Birds of Britain and Europe* (Hamlyn, 1970).
Cramp, *et al* (eds), *Handbook of the Birds of Europe the Middle East and North Africa* – Volumes 1–4 (Oxford University Press, 1977–1985).

Shoot Management
Coats, A. *The Amateur Keeper* (Andre Deutsch, 1989)
Coles, C. L. (ed.), *The Complete Book of Game Conservation* (Stanley Paul & Co., 1984, 3rd edition)
The Game Conservancy Trust – Green Guides Series:
No. 2 Ponds and Lakes for Wildfowl (1993)
No. 4 Wild Partridge Management (1992)
No. 8 Gamebird Rearing (1994)
No. 14 Game in Winter (Feeding and Management) (1986)
No. 15 Woodlands for Pheasants (1988)
No. 18 Red-legged Partridges (1983)
No. 10 Gamebird Releasing (1996)
No. 16 Predation Control (1994)
McCall, I., *Your Shoot, Gamekeeping and Management* (A&C Black, 1990, 2nd edition)

Game and Wildfowl Biology

Hill, D. A. and Robertson, P., *The Pheasant, Ecology, Management and Conservation* (BSP Professional Books, 1988)

McKelvie, C. L., *A Future for Game?* (Unwin, 1985)

McKelvie, C. L., *The Book of the Woodcock* (Swan Hill Press, 1990)

Owen, M., *Wildfowl of Europe* (Macmillan, 1977)

Potts, G. R., *The Partridge, Pesticides, Predation and Conservation* (Collins, 1986)

Robertson, P. A. *A Natural History of the Pheasant.* (Swan Hill Press, 1997)

Vesey-Fitzgerald, B., *British Game* (Collins, 1946)

Gundogs

Cox, G, and Deeley, M., *Getting it Right with Gundogs* (The Game Conservancy Trust, 1987)

Deeley, M., *Working Gundogs* (Crowood, 1989)

Deeley, M., *Advanced Gundog Training.* (Crowood, 1990)

Douglas, J., *Complete Gundog Training Manual* (Swan Hill Press, 2003)

Irving, J., *Professional Gundog Training* (Swan Hill Press, 2006)

Moxon, P. R. A., *Gundogs: Training and Field Trials* (Swan Hill Press, 2006)

Moxon, P. R. A., *Training the Roughshooter's Dog* (Swan Hill Press, 1977)

Stephens, W., *Gundog Sense and Sensibility* (Swan Hill Press, 2001)

Learning to Shoot

BASC *Handbook of Shooting – The Sporting Shotgun.* (Swan Hill Press, 2000)

Coles, C. L. (ed) *Shooting and Stalking, A Basic Guide* (Stanley Paul, 1988, revised edition)

Stanbury, P. and Carlisle, G. L., *Clay Pigeon Marksmanship* (Stanley Paul, 1974)

Yardley, M., *BASC Guide to Shooting Game* (Swan Hill Press, 2007)

Rough Shooting and the Law

Frost, D., *Sporting Firearms and the Law* (BFSS, 1997)

Parkes, C. and Thornley, J., *Fair Game: The Law of Country Sports and the Protection of Wildlife* (Pelham, 2000)

Rough Shooting, Narrative and Instruction

Begbie, E., *Fowler in the Wild* (David and Charles, 1987)

Brander, M., *A Concise Guide to Game Shooting* (Sportsman's Press, 1989)

Brander, M., *The Sporting Roughshoot* (Pelham, 1989)

Cadman, W. A., *Tales of a Wildfowler* (Collins, 1957)

Cadman, W. A., *Shoulder Gunning for Duck* (*Shooting Times* Library, Percival Marshall, 1962)

Catlin, C., *The Game Book* (Swan Hill Press, 2007)

Coats, A., *Pigeon Shooting* (Andre Deutsch, 1990, new edition)

Humphreys J., *Hides, Calls and Decoys* (Percival Marshall, 1978)

Humphreys J., *Shooting Pigeons* (David & Charles, 1988)

Marchington, J. E., *The Complete Shot* (A & C Black, 1981)

Marchington, J. E., *The Practical Wildfowler* (A & C Black, 1977)

Marchington, J. E., *The History of Wildfowling* (A & C Black, 1980)

McKay, J., *The Ferret and Ferreting Handbook* (Crowood, 1989)

Pitman, I., *And Clouds Flying* (Faber, 1947)

Savory, A., *Norfolk Fowler* (Geoffrey Bles, 1953)

Swan, M. C., *Fowling for Duck* (Crowood, 1988)

Walsingham, Lord and Sir R. Payne-Gallwey, *Shooting (Field and Covert)* (The Badminton Library, Longman, 1887)

Walsingham, Lord and Sir R. Payne-Gallwey, *Shooting (Moor and Marsh)* (The Badminton Library, Longman, 1887)

Game Cookery

Coats, P., *Prue's New Country Kitchen* (Colt Books, 1997)

Coats, P., *The Poacher's Cookbook* (White Lion Books, 1999, 3rd edition)

Jardine-Paterson, V., *Good Game* (Swan Hill Press, 2002)

Thompson, B., *Game and Fish Cookbook* (Swan Hill Press, 2002)

Index

binoculars 24–5
bismuth shot 40, 100

calls/calling 51–2
camouflage 19–21, 47, 143–6
Canada geese 37, 56, 111, 117–8
cartridge belts 49–50
cartridge extractors 50
cartridges 35, 38–42, 50
choke 38
clothing and footwear 19–20, 46–8, 132,
    133–4
codes of conduct 45, 60, 71, 125
cold weather
    bans 173
    and game feeding 171–3
    movements 111
collared doves 56, 127
conservation
    conserving stocks 59, 73–4, 83–4, 124,
        149–53, 170
    habitat improvement 78, 149–50,
        154–63
conservation through wise use 26

decoys
    and decoying 135–43
    pigeon shooting 130–2, 137
    selecting 138–40
    sighting 122, 138–41
    shyness 143
dogs
    care of 32
    choosing 29–32
    in the field 29–34, 67, 80, 97, 105–6

    training 19, 32–4
driven game shooting 11, 71–4, 81–3, 91,
    97–9, 106–7
ducks
    calling 51, 140
    decoys 139–41, 142–3
    driving 124–5
    feeding habits 22–3, 113–6
    flighting patterns 22–3, 112–3, 115,
        118–123
    hand-reared 124, 162

ferrets 107–8
field sports organisations 173, 175–6
firearms certificates 41, 54
flight ponds
    feeding 121–2, 173
    management 158–60
    shooting 120–2
fox control 167–9

gadwall 56, 114
game licences 58
game bags 49–50
geese
    calling 51–2
    decoys 119, 136–7
    driving 124–5
    feeding habits 112, 117–8
    flighting patterns 112–3, 117–20, 123
    shot size 35, 38
goldeneye 56, 116
grey partridge 55, 75–83, 150–1, 158
greylag geese 56, 117–8

guns
 care of 43–4, 50–1
 choice of 40–3
 how they work 35–7
 over and under 42
 proof 43
 pump action 41
 safe use 44–5
 semi-automatic 41
 side by side 42

habitat management
 hedgerows 156–8
 wetlands 149–50, 158–60, 162
 woodland 149, 154–6, 163
hand-reared birds 65, 83, 149–53, 161–2
hanging, dressing and cooking
   game 49, 127, 177–8
hares 57, 103–4, 106
hearing protection 48–9
hedgerow management 156–8
hides 143–6

insurance 58–9

knives 50

Larsen trap 167
law
 cold weather 173
 firearms certificate 41, 54
 game licences 58
 non-toxic shot 39–40, 58, 100, 125
 open seasons 55–8
 shoot leases 54–5, 101, 126
 shotgun certificates 53–4
 Sunday shooting 57–8

mallard 36, 56, 111, 113–4, 142

night shooting 24, 123
noise 19, 21, 67, 123–4
non-toxic shot
 bismuth 40, 100
 general 15, 39–40, 58, 100, 125
 steel 39
 tin 40
 tungsten 40

open seasons 55–8
open country 75–6, 158

over shooting 59, 73–4, 83–4, 124,
   149–53, 170

partridges
 driving 81–3
 habitat 75–8, 158
 habits 78
 hand-reared 76–7, 78–9, 150
 origins 75
 shooting 55, 78–84
pest species 56, 101, 104, 126–30
pheasants
 'cocks only' 74–5
 driving 71–3
 habitat 65–7, 149, 154–6, 163
 habits 65–7
 hand-reared 63–5, 150–3
 origins 63–5
 shooting 55, 65, 67–74
pigeons
 and decoys 130–2, 133, 136–9, 142–3
 feeding habits 126–30, 139
 identification 26, 126–7
 shooting 20, 21, 56, 130–4
pinkfooted geese 26, 56, 111, 117–8
pintail 56, 114–5
poaching and trespass 54–5, 58
pochard 56, 116
pointers 12–13, 15, 30, 90
predators 164–9
public attitudes to shooting 20–1, 25, 49,
   60, 134, 160–3, 164

quarry identification 24–26

rabbits 57, 101–3, 104–9
range – shotgun 35–43, 59, 131–2
red-legged partridge 55, 75–83
restocking 65, 83, 150–3, 161–2
retrievers 30, 80, 97
roost shooting 21–2, 132–4

safety
 angles 45
 glasses 49
 handling guns 43, 44–5, 59
 hearing 48–9
 insurance 58–9
 keeping guns 54
 shooting 44–5, 83
 shooting ground game 108–9

shoot management
  conserving stocks 59, 73–4, 83–4,
      149–53, 170
  feeding 171–3
  habitat 149–50, 154–63
  predation control 164–9
  restocking 65, 83, 150–3, 161–2
shoot leases 54–5, 101, 126
shooting seasons 55–58
shot sizes 35, 38–40, 99–100, 108–9
shotgun certificate 53–4
shoveler 56, 115–6
snipe
  driving 97–8
  habitat 94–6, 149–50
  habits 94–6
  shooting 55, 96–100
  shot size 39, 40, 99–100
spaniels 29–30, 90
spring feeding 171–3
stealth in the field 19–21, 48, 67, 134
steel shot 44
stock doves 26, 127
Sunday shooting 57–8

teal 23, 56, 114–5, 121
tin shot 40
tufted duck 56, 116

tunnel trap 168–9
turtle dove 127
tungsten shot 40

wetland management 149–50, 158–60,
    161–2
whitefronted geese 56, 111, 117–8
wigeon 23, 56, 112, 115, 118, 142
wildfowl
  driving 124–5
  feeding habits 22–3, 112–13, 118–23
  flighting patterns 22–3, 112–13,
    118–23
  migration patterns 59, 111
  recognition 22–3
  walking up 25, 123–4
wildfowling bans 173
winter feeding 171–3
woodpigeons – see pigeons
woodcock
  ageing 93
  driving 91
  flight lines 22, 86, 91–3
  habitat 85–8, 154
  habits 22, 85–9
  shooting 56, 59, 89–93
woodland management 149, 154–6, 163
wounded game 36–40, 51, 122, 124